Of Love and Of Suffering

Books by ROBERT E. FITCH
Published by THE WESTMINSTER PRESS

Of Love and Of Suffering
Shakespeare: The Perspective of Value

OF LOVE AND
OF SUFFERING

preface to Christian Ethics
for Heathen Philosophers

by **Robert E. Fitch**

with a postscript
for Heathen Theologians

THE WESTMINSTER PRESS · Philadelphia

ISBN 0-664-24892-6

LIBRARY OF CONGRESS CATALOG CARD No. 73-115821

PUBLISHED BY THE WESTMINSTER PRESS ®
PHILADELPHIA, PENNSYLVANIA

PRINTED IN THE UNITED STATES OF AMERICA

Contents

PREFACE *for Heathen Philosophers*

When, after teaching philosophy for twenty years, I was at last promoted, as I like to say, to become a theologian, I experienced a psychic trauma from which I have not since recovered and from which, indeed, I hope never to recover. All those twenty years I had been teaching a course in ethics. Yet all during that time there had been no word in the textbook, no mention in class, no discussion at meetings of the American Philosophical Association of two affairs which poets, mystics, saints, novelists, dramatists, historians, recognize as among the basic facts of life—namely, love and suffering.

As far as philosophy is primarily an enterprise of reason, this is bound to be the case. The reasonable thing to do is what Aristotle does in the *Nicomachean Ethics*—concentrate on friendship, since friendship, unlike love, is amenable to rational controls. It is true that there is eloquent discourse about love in Plato and in Schopenhauer. But the first elevates love to ethereal delights, while the second debases it to carnal appetites: neither one is able to effect a union of the flesh and the spirit. Furthermore, when philosophers begin to translate love into social ethics, they set up an ideal of community which is either totalitarian or anarchistic, or which, as in Rousseau, plays back and forth from one pole to the other. Curiously enough, it is precisely this paradoxical and intolerable form of community which is much touted by the small revolutionary segment of American youth today.

As for suffering—with the exception of Schopenhauer, who consciously borrowed from Oriental religions—this is hardly known at all to the philosophers. In the traditions of the Cyrenaics and of the Epicureans, what is done with suffering is to trivialize it under the title of pain. Of course the Stoics understood the value of suffering as a kind of allopathic medicine for the softness of the soul. But there is no clear apprehension of the difference between the pain of the hedonists and the suffering of the religionists until we come to the British Utilitarians. One must applaud the honesty if not the spiritual sensitivity of Jeremy Bentham, who acknowledged that, in defiance of all good sense, there is a peculiar portion of humanity which prefers to live by the "theological principle," or the "principle of asceticism," according to which suffering is a higher value than pleasure.

Indeed, it is only the great religions—Judaism, Christianity, Buddhism—which can tell us about love and suffering. The ethical values in a rationalistic tradition are wisdom, duty, pleasure, power. When the religious tradition and the philosophic tradition have not completely come apart—as with the classical Greeks, the Stoics, and Immanuel Kant—then wisdom and duty are elaborated for us with deep insight. But when philosophy turns consciously and rigorously atheistic, as in Lucretius and Hobbes, its values are pleasure and power. If in this writing I lump all these philosophers together under a rubric of heathenism, my intention—not altogether invidious—

is simply to indicate that they come outside the controlling influence of a religious heritage.

Unfortunately philosophy today has become an inordinately inbred discipline. The apostles of linguistic analysis find that they can talk only about talking, and end up by talking only to themselves. The positivists assure us that all questions of value are purely emotive in character, and that what ordinary mortals regard as the most meaningful of questions are in fact meaningless questions. However, if we leave these two sects to their own autistic rituals, there is still the great and variegated tradition of the history of philosophy that runs from Socrates down to Dewey, Whitehead, Russell, and the existentialists. I am always grateful that for a while I was permitted to be an acolyte in the temple of this tradition. For it was here that I learned much that could not be learned in a tradition purely theological. And I beg the reader to remark that, when I cite some source other than the Biblical, it is usually from this same heritage of heathen philosophy.

In a quest for the meanings of love and of suffering, it was fortunate that I had early shaped my interests as a devotee of the theater. The Athenian dramatists, Shakespeare, Corneille, Racine, Molière, and then the great moderns of the nineteenth and twentieth centuries, all have a deal to say about what concerns us here. This part of my pilgrimage has taken me to the theater in Paris, London, New York, and San Francisco, and, at assorted festivals, has enabled me to see some 150 productions onstage of the plays of Shakespeare. If the immediately contemporary theater appears to be more enraptured with lust than with love, and with a diabolical sadomasochism rather than with significant suffering, then it must be said that here is where a retreat to the past brings us closer to reality than does a mindless immersion in the sensations of the moment.

While this book is an essay on the meanings of love and of suffering, it requires to be said most emphatically that it is in no sense an adequate treatise on social ethics. Here I find it a bit curious that, while my lifelong concern has been with social ethics, I begin to look now to the more personal problem. Actually it was an existential rediscovery of the great Hebrew prophets that, at a certain point in my career, brought me back from a spell of atheism to being once again a professed believer in Biblical Christianity. But to my great astonishment it was when I was in service as a chaplain on an attack transport in World War II, when I had supposed that now the prophets would speak to me again with renewed force, that I found myself turning directly to the Jesus of the New Testament for insight and for strength. Certainly there is no simple transition from love to justice, but love lies at the heart of any tolerable system of justice. In our time, moreover, it is necessary to go down deep and to find the root of reality. For me this means that, as I become more radical on social issues, I become more conservative in morals.

The revolution that goes on about us at this moment, above all in the establishment of the civil rights of the black man, makes all the more poignant the problem of the values of love and of suffering. I have never been a practicing pacifist and am not an absolutist, as this text will show, even with a doctrine of Christian love. Nevertheless, Martin Luther King, Jr., like Mahatma Gandhi before him, has shown us how the spirit of love may be conjoined with a passion for social justice. The deliberate effort to denigrate (how ironical does that word ring today!) King after his death, to play him down as an Uncle Tom, as a mere apostle of patient endurance, is one of the scandalous episodes in American history. It may be that, toward the end, he was due for a change in tactics. But it was never true that he was losing his grip. A King or a Gandhi does not lose his grip even when he is supposed to be dead. As for those persons, black or white, who follow the way of four-letter-word incantations accompanied by flamboyant outbursts of violence, there is no evidence that they manage to promote anything other than reaction and suppression and perhaps a new tyranny. For in the end as at the beginning it is only love that liberates.

The test of what is said in these pages is first of all empirical. Is it or is it not the case that love and suffering are two of the great facts of life? Does or does not this writing treat of those facts in an honest and an adequate manner? If in the pursuit of these affairs I prefer denotations to definitions, I can only plead that I have lived now for some time with my wife, and that I have not yet been able to encompass her in a definition, but somehow she appears to be more real to me than an isosceles triangle. If one must follow classical models in getting at the nitty-gritty of the moral life, then I have a partiality for Socrates and his plain examples from everyday, for Aristotle and his great portraits in the *Nicomachean Ethics,* for Epictetus and his vivid involvement in the give-and-take of ethical inquiry about our human concerns. In these thinkers we have a practicing empiricism often more genuine than what is to be found among professing empiricists.

But if the initial test is empirical, the final test is pragmatic. Historic empiricism fell into two errors. Starting out as the appeal to fact and to experience, it soon substituted a formula for experience, and then pulverized that experience. It also ignored that large part of human experience which is history. These are faults which one finds in the British empiricists, ancient and modern. William James and John Dewey are free from the first fault, but are not exempt from the second. Only Reinhold Niebuhr has kept free from these corruptions. What is needed, then, is an historically minded pragmatism—one that is experimental enough to project itself into the future as it is wise enough to draw on the wisdom of the past. Inescapably in ethics the test of consequences on the whole and in the long run is the definitive test. Or as a more ancient authority has said, "By their fruits ye shall know them."

R. E. F.

Pacific School of Religion
Berkeley, California

1

The Choice to Love

There is a choice that every man must make. It is the choice to love or to hate. This is the first choice, though it is not the last. There are also choices of the objects of love, of motives and means and ends, of the rules that make the game worth the playing, of the allies that will bear up human love against its own frailties, of the ordeals that shall be willingly undergone to fulfill love's purposes, of the comfort and of the cross which are the reward and the price of the enterprise of love. Yet this first choice must be made. To seek to evade it by blowing now hot and now cold is to destroy the self.

For to be afraid to love is the greatest cowardice that can befall a man. And if we mean to love, then we have to get at it as Bergson said we do in our first effort to swim. We do not start with a definition, or with a logical demonstration that love is a good. We take the plunge. Our first question, therefore, is not "What is love?" or "How is love possible?", but "Where do we begin?"

THE LADDER OR THE LEAP

One approach to the problem makes use of the symbol of the ladder of love. We begin where we are, with the lowest and nearest object of love, and ascend a step at a time to the highest and worthiest object of love. This theory is linked with a genetic psychology which says that everyone begins with the love of himself, then turns to a love of members of the same sex, next to a love of members of the opposite sex, until he has finally taken in the full range of human loves. Besides the symbol of the ladder, one could use the symbol of a series of concentric circles, so that one moves from the love of self to the love of family, to the love of community, to the love of country, to the love of humanity, and at last to the love of God. This is also called the educational approach, since it makes clear the various stages in a rational pedagogy of love.

However, experience indicates that one step does not automatically lead to the next step, and that the intermediate steps are not always necessary to get from the first to the last. A Don Juan or a Casanova becomes a master of heterosexual love on the purely sensual level, but then goes no farther. On the other hand, some of the great lovers of truth, or of humanity, or of God—a Socrates, an Abraham Lincoln, a Saint Francis—have not been distinguished for their success in marital relations. If it were true that you must first do well with a love at hand before you can move on to a remoter love, then none of these would have made it. Indeed, it is arguable, in the case of a John Wesley, that his frustration in his own marriage was a factor in forcing him to embrace a larger loyalty, and that, in the case of the prophet Hosea, it was the ordeal of his own unhappy home that helped him to envisage better the ordeal of a loving and a suffering God.

One danger of the approach to love by way of the lad-der is complacency. There is the disposition to make an idolatry of whatever love gives us an immediate satisfac-tion, and to lose all desire to move on to other loves. Many readers of the New Testament feel that Jesus is less than cordial in the way he speaks of the family.[1] This is because he wished to give ethical definition to the family, and also to stress the higher loyalty to God that must take prece-dence over our loyalty to the family. In the culture in which he lived a devotion to the family, or the clan, might get in the way of larger affections. Certainly the love of one's family, like the love of one's country, is a love of the good. But, when we turn it into an idolatry, we shut our-selves off from higher loves, and begin to corrupt the very love which we pretend to cherish the most.

The gravest danger in the approach to love by the ladder is the danger of a disillusionment that turns to cyni-cism and back to narcissism. Every significant adventure in life is fraught with the peril of a hurt to oneself. In-deed, we may say that this hurt is a certainty in love. If a young man like Hamlet is bitterly disillusioned in his love for his mother, he finds it natural to project his dis-illusionment onto the innocent Ophelia, and then onto women in general. If a young girl has her feelings wounded in her first step toward going steady with a young man, she may be tempted to recoil into herself and to say, "Every man is a scoundrel." Thus a cynic is a person who has been disillusioned in his love of all else but still manages to be in love with himself. Cynicism, in its absence of humility and charity and in its egotistical presumptions, is altogether incompatible with love. The punishment of the cynic is that he must end up by hating himself. For no self can long love a self that finally loves none other than the self. There is nothing there to love.

Besides the educational approach of the ladder there is the mystical approach of the leap of love. In this case, we begin with the highest instead of the lowest; or, if you like, begin at the end instead of at the beginning. We begin with the love of God, and from there reach back to our lesser loves. The symbol of the ladder appeals to what is rational and pedestrian in our natures. The symbol of the leap appeals to what is imaginative and jet-propelled in our impulses. Also, if we are concerned with a sound pedagogy, there can be no question but that, however it may be with adults who have succumbed to utility, small children, on the other hand, are able easily to make the leap of faith that takes them direct to a personal God. A student in college or in seminary may need a lot of theology and exegesis before he can understand the Lord's Prayer. A child may apprehend its basic meaning at once by an act of the imagination.

This direct leap of faith to the love of God, nevertheless, has its own danger. And it may be in recognition of this danger that some famous mystics have been concerned to clarify the intermediate stages in a ladder of love to God. Because one can become so intoxicated with the love of God that the enjoyment of that love turns into the auto-erotic indulgence of the spiritual voluptuary. Then we are back once more to narcissism, only this time it has a halo about its head. So we are warned that "if a man says, 'I love God,' while hating his brother, he is a liar."[2] There is too much in the literature of so-called mysticism that is little more than a caressing of the soul for its more pretentious vanities and aspirations. Here we have just the self confronting the self's God, while the other selves in the world vanish from consciousness, and God's own self is gradually gobbled up into the maw of an insatiable Me.

Yet if it is the true God that we love, and not some idol, then that highest love can lend both quality and dynamic to all our lesser loves. The First Epistle of John speaks well when it tells us that he who loves God must also love his brother, but perhaps it is confusing priorities when it says of a man that "If he does not love the brother whom he has seen, it cannot be that he loves God whom he has not seen."[3] For men see by the eye of faith as well as by the eye of flesh, and it may be precisely the vision of the God we have known only by faith that enables us best to love the man or the woman we have known in the flesh. So a person may love his family under God, and love it without idolatry for what is good in it, and with a faithfulness that is stronger than what is weak in it. Again a man may love his country under God, as did Hosea and Jeremiah, and cherish every excellence that is in it, and yet remain loyal to it when it denies and defeats its own excellence.

Finally, then, if it be asked again, "Where do we begin to love?" the honest answer must be that we can begin here, or there, or anywhere. For if this really is God's world, there is no part of it that may not lead to other parts of it and at last to God himself, and there is no part of the Creator that may not lead to his several creatures. If man is that one of God's creatures who can walk and even run, and also mount up with wings as an eagle, then man needs the instruction of his reason and the satisfaction of his imagination. He needs steps for security; he needs a leap for adventure. Yet let no man pretend that he can encompass all loves, for only God can do that. And

wherever a man may chance to begin his lovings, let him
make sure that the range of his loves takes in objects that
are both high and humble: for both God and man's
brother are near at hand; neither one is closer or farther
away than the other.

THE ORDERING OF OUR LOVES

While we may begin anywhere in our acts of loving,
it is yet inescapable that we must establish some pattern
of priorities in our loves. The injunction of the Scriptures
is clear. It does not say, like some contemporary schools
of psychotherapy: "Thou shalt love thyself with all thy
heart and with all thy soul and with all thy mind. This
is the first and great commandment. Next you should
love your neighbor; and at last you might love your God,
if you manage to get around to it." The Scriptures have a
realistic assessment of human nature; they take for
granted that man does a pretty good job of loving himself. So the second commandment reads, "Thou shalt love
thy neighbor as thyself." However, the great commandment, which comes first in any ordering of our loves,
reads, "Thou shalt love the Lord thy God with all thy
heart, and with all thy soul, and with all thy mind."[4]
When our loves are disordered, it creates a schism in
the soul. There is an old teaching that man by his very
nature is a spiritual schismatic: the body against the
mind, the flesh against the spirit, the heart against the
head, the multitude of impulses, appetites, and desires
against the rule of reason. Even Saint Paul complains,
"The good which I want to do, I fail to do; but what I do
is the wrong which is against my will."[5] This classical
dualism, however, may be a bit too simple as a descrip-

tion of modern man. For man today is in a manifold
predicament in which he suffers a scatteration of selves,
all of which pull in diverse directions as they are drawn
by disordered and loose-ended loves. Such a man might
pray to God, "O unite my soul in the love of Thee!"[6]

One way of ordering our loves is in a vertical hierarchy.
Here we are called upon to decide on a sequence of loves
in which one love, in case of conflict, must take prece-
dence over another. Thus one might order one's love of
self, of family, of community, of country, of humanity, of
God, in a hierarchical scheme. The usual assumption
would be that the lesser love agrees with the higher love
and actually ministers to it. So what I do to help myself
or to strengthen my home must also help the community
in which I live and strengthen the nation of which I am
a citizen. But there is no simple preestablished harmony
here, and there will be critical moments when I have to
choose to injure one love in order to exalt another. There
is no tidy codification of loyalties which can delete the
imperative to make sacrifices.

Another way to speak of how we order our loves is to
say that the arrangement is personal and horizontal. Let
it be granted that there is a hierarchy in our loves, and
that much of the time these several loves interact with
and minister to one another. The real problem, however,
is one of allocating times, and occasions, and energies.
Should we set aside particular seasons for the worship of
God, for playing with the children, for being good pa-
triots, for diligence in the daily task, for the exercise of
civic responsibilities, for rest and recreation? It is easy
to make fun of our pietist ancestors for the meticulous
way in which they plotted a day's routine in eating, sleep-
ing, prayer, work, philanthropy, and sometimes even a

little fun. But if we merely yield to the pressures as they come to us, we are soon guilty of neglecting some of our most fundamental loyalties.

One thing, in any case, is clear: the object of our supreme love is our god. This is the object for which we care the most, which we really worship, and to which, in a showdown, we give precedence over everything else. Tillich calls it the object of ultimate concern. In the story of the temptation in the wilderness the devil tries Jesus to see what it is that Jesus really wants out of life. The devil's first appearance is in the form of a Marxian economic determinist: he suggests that Jesus turn the stones into bread in order to fill the bellies of men. The next temptation is a thrust at spiritual pride: let Jesus make a public and spectacular demonstration of his very special connections with the deity. In the third temptation the devil speaks the language of Machiavelli: let Jesus take authority over all the kingdoms of the world. But Jesus' answer is clear: "It is written, Thou shalt worship the Lord thy God, and him only shalt thou serve."[7]

Just who or what is the object of supreme love which is the god of the American people? A few years ago it was said that, because we live in an acquisitive society, our god is Mammon. Now that we live in an affluent society, it is not clear that we are suddenly emancipated from "the deceitfulness of riches."[8] We glorify the consumer rather than the producer; we practice deficit financing, and live beyond our incomes as individuals and as a nation; we begin to despise the old-fashioned work ethic and to assume that some foreign entity, some special class of helots, must owe us a living. More and more we dwell in a world of fiscal fantasies. Even those who affect most to be in rebellion against "the system," the hippie and the hoodlum, are themselves the pestilential effluvium of an affluent society. Our biggest hypocrisy is to pretend that we are a very idealistic generation, with no care for material ends; but that is because we take it for granted that the material basis for our comfortable society will always be provided by the grace of the god Mammon. Yet this sort of analysis, which follows the naïve monism of the economic determinist, probably gives us too simple a picture. It is more likely that Americans today are polytheists, who no longer know the true God from the tin gods, and have forgotten the art of ordering their loves.

When we have found and ordered our loves, then the important thing is to give ourselves to them as generously as we know how. We are not to use them for what we can get out of them. We are to serve them for what we can creatively do in our calling. What is so sorry in the account of Ecclesiastes is that the author tries everything —wisdom, wealth, women, children, goodness, power— but he never really loves anything but himself. These others are merely tools to titillate his own ego with its appetites. So it is that he manages the reverse miracle of turning bread into stones. For him rightfully all is vanity. But for a self-giving love, life is a glory even though it come at the price of a cross, provided one has loved worthily with all his heart and all his soul and all his mind.

THE UNIQUE IN CHRISTIAN LOVE

Perhaps now we can inquire more closely about the character of this Christian love to which we are supposed to give ourselves with such abandon. What is unique and distinctive about it?

First of all, the sort of love being discussed here belongs peculiarly to the Christian tradition. The best teaching in Greek philosophy, found in Aristotle's *Nicomachean Ethics*, upholds the ideal of friendship, which is elaborated in considerable detail. In the Jewish tradition the chief emphasis is on justice and on righteousness, although the beginnings of the teaching of love are found in Hosea and in Jeremiah, and Jesus of course was in the line of the great Hebrew prophets. In a Confucian scheme the essential is courtesy or benevolence. For the Moslem what matters is a practical and disciplined philanthropy. Mahayana Buddhism, with its ideal of sympathy and compassion, comes very close to the Christian ideal, but it stands against a background of pessimism about this world which is contrary to the Biblical affirmation of the value and importance of our life in history. Only in the New Testament is the teaching of love made explicit and also fully incarnate in a person.

Another feature of Christian love is that it is a command to the will rather than to the affections. One might ask, "How can you command love?" Part of the answer is that God can command it if man cannot. But the other part of the answer, which is rooted in an Old Testament and Jewish doctrine of the nature of the self, reminds us that we can give orders to our wills when we cannot constrain our feelings. What the commandment requires us to do is to act in a loving way toward others. Whether or not we feel like doing so is a secondary question. There may be cases, as in the arranged marriages in parts of the Old World, where it takes the feelings a little time to catch up with the will. For Schopenhauer, of course, all this was monstrous and hypocritical. He assailed an equivalent teaching in Kant without being aware that this was also the Biblical teaching. Schopenhauer liked to declare *operari sequitur esse*—what you do depends on what you are. A Biblical Christian would have to reverse that and say *esse sequitur operari*—what you are flows from what you do.

This brings us to a third consideration, which is that Christian love transcends liking, respect, mutuality, reciprocity. There is a *New Yorker* cartoon which shows two very puzzled students, in clerical collars, walking together along the inner court of a theological seminary. Says one of them, "What gets me about this place is that they want you to love people you don't even like." That is precisely the point. In the ordinary relations of romantic love between a man and a woman, it is assumed that liking and respect are minimal ingredients. Indeed, the absence of self-respect and of mutual respect is part of what defines the difference between infatuation and real love. But while the ideal of Christian love is always relevant to courtship and to marriage, it goes beyond them in that it does not depend upon personal preferences, or even upon love returned, but is wider in scope and bolder in vision. This command to love is God's categorical imperative to man.

Also, as Christian love goes beyond mutuality, it declares that the important thing is to give love, not to receive love. Certainly there is no prohibition against love that is returned. When we do receive from another a response in love, we can be grateful for it. But it is health to go about giving love; it is sickness to go about wanting to be loved. One may have a desire for a fellowship in love that is positive in stressing the shared activities of a creative and outgoing impulse. Yet the inordinate passion to be loved, whether in a private person

or in a public official, reveals itself as predatory and imperialistic and more eager to receive than to give. Doubtless there are cases in psychotherapy when the first thing
that needs to be done is to give love to one who has never
known it. But the therapy will be of no help unless it
goes beyond commiserating and compassionating. The
patient is not well again until he has been put in a position
where he gives rather than receives love. This ability to
give love is the power of healing for ourselves as much as
for others, which we always have within us.

Finally, for Christian love the cross is always the criterion. The cross is foolishness to those like Nietzsche
who look for a power that tramples down the weak and
rejoices with the strong. The cross is a stumbling block to
all those who put their faith in goodwill and right reason
as sufficient to redeem us from our errors. But the cross,
whether it is full with the burden of a Christ in agony, or
empty as the symbol of a Christ in triumph, is a reminder
of the last ordeal of love, which is always the ordeal of
suffering. And the Servant of this love comes to us, not
wreathed in roses, but with a crown of thorns on his head.

2

Love at Work

Now that we have had a look at some of the preliminary features of love, it is necessary to call for more precise information. Just what are the motives to love? What are the modes of behavior in which love shows itself? And what are the rewards, if any, of a love that gives itself at the price of a cross in transcendence of the demand for love returned?

THE MOTIVES TO LOVE

After all, why should we bother with people? One of the classical answers, which comes to us from romanticism, is that persons are inherently precious. This is often formulated as the doctrine of the sacredness of personality. Just what the "ality" adds to the "person" is not quite clear, since there are some persons who, in the ordinary usage of the term, do not have much "personality." We might better speak, then, of the sacredness of the self. This lies at the basis of a child-centered curriculum in education, of a client-centered psychotherapy with its nondirective techniques, of a self-centered course

of conduct in political action in which the concern for the
release of pent-up feelings is more important than a concern for social well-being. In general this makes for an
ethics in which the permissive is more prominent than
the imperative. Much of this philosophy, from Rousseau
through Pestalozzi to John Dewey, rules in our elementary
schools.

Another classical answer, which comes from rationalism,
says that the divine in man is his reason. This view of life
is regnant in our colleges and universities. It affirms, with
Aristotle, that all men by nature desire to know. It is the
intellect that raises us above the brutes, that makes us
akin to the gods. Reason is our redeemer. It is reason that
explains mysteries, reason that solves problems. The way
to resolve tensions between persons or between nations
is through rational discussion and negotiation. The way
to bring about a better world is through intelligent plan-
ning. As for those who do not care to take part in the
life of reason, we have to say, with Aristotle, that they are
simply subhuman. So he argued that natural slaves are
naturally irrational beings; that children are creatures
who have not yet come to maturity in intelligence; and
that women are people who have enough reason to understand the ideas of their menfolk, but not enough reason
to think for themselves. Thus rationalism is incorrigibly
aristocratic, as romanticism is anarchically democratic.

If our candidate for being loved manages to get through
school and college, and to move out into the larger world
of affairs, he will encounter another doctrine of human
nature. This is materialism, which says that we should
pay respect to the successful man for whatever he embodies of power, prestige, and possessions. For persons
who like to think they are realists this is the one doctrine

of man with which we must reckon. According to the temper of the times there can be variations as to which one of the gods in a materialistic pantheon is assigned the chief place. Some years ago we were in love with prosperity; more recently we cared for security; but currently we worship power, with a quiet decorum if we have it, but with a savage lustfulness if we still lack it and must seek after it. And there is no doubt that materialism contains its truth. If it is sensuality for man to think he can live by bread alone, it is pride to think he can despise his daily bread.

There are other doctrines of human nature, but these three are the ones that divide our allegiance now. A couple of things are to be said about them. Each of these views is inadequate and self-defeating in practice. The romantic who is brought up to believe that he is entitled to his bottle whenever he cries for it is going to be bitterly frustrated by a world that does not readily cater to his desires. The rationalist must learn that in some of the great adventures of life—religion, politics, matrimony, war —reason is a tool in the hands of something mightier than itself. The materialist will make the disillusioning discovery that, while he adores prestige and prosperity, he has no secret for attaining to them, and that those who are really successful in the pursuit subscribe to another creed. Again, nothing inherently lovable comes out of this kind of creature. The romantic degenerates too rapidly into the insufferable, spoiled brat. The rationalist decays into the skeptic or into the apostle of the absurd. The materialist reverts to the beast in the jungle. Indeed, if we love people just for their selves, or for their intellects, or for their possessions, we shall soon be falling out of love with them.

The Christian teaching as to why we should love persons rests upon two affirmations. One is that man is he for whom Christ died. So we love others because God first loved us.[1] This declares God's act in history, and exhibits his concern for our careers on this earth. The other affirmation, which Christians share with Jews, is that man is a child of God, made in the image of God. This human being affirmed by Christian faith contains as part of himself all that is cherished by the other doctrines of man. As an historical being, he is a union of body and soul, and what is material matters to him as much as what is spiritual. As a child of God he shares in a capacity for intelligence, freedom, and love, and also has an immortal worth and dignity. But man is also a creature of frailty and finitude, who is corrupted by sin; and he can reject his responsibility in history, debase his reason, pollute his affections, and destroy his liberty. If we are going to continue to love him, it will have to be not just for what we see in fact but for what we believe by faith.

Let us be quite clear at this point about the affinities and the differences between a secular and a Christian view of man. Christianity is just as much concerned with the self, with reason, and with prosperity as is any other view. Indeed, it claims that the only way to affirm the sacredness of the person, to further the prosperity of man, to promote the pursuits of reason, is within the framework of the Christian vision. After all, it was Voltaire's Candide who, after a long and tough pilgrimage, came to the conclusion *"Travaillons sans raisonner*—Let us work without thinking!" But Bunyan's Christian, throughout a long and tough pilgrimage, continues incessant in reasoning, because his intellect has something worthwhile to believe in.

The prime motive, then, for a Christian to love his fellowman is an act of faith. This faith is an experimental one, and is therefore tested by its fruits. But it is a faith which goes beyond an immediate empiricism, beyond the evidence that lies just below your nose. Because man— let us confess it—can act in a most unlovable way. And if we persist in loving him, it is because we hold to a faith which is the substance of things hoped for, the evidence of things not seen.[2]

THE MODES OF LOVE

How does man's love show itself? Does it have modes of behavior that, in the language of Dewey, are public, observable, and verifiable? The best answer to this question lies in the analogy between God's love and man's love. God is known as Creator, Judge, and Redeemer.

The creative activity of love is its primary function. This impact of love upon others is provocative or evocative in its effects. So the child has an understanding parent who helps him along the way; or the student finds a teacher who brings out the best in him; or the writer discovers an editor who challenges him to do what he did not know he had it in him to do. A good track coach, a business executive, a political leader, the pastor of a church—any one of these may have the seeing eye that discerns unsuspected potentialities in others, or may have the peculiar quality of personality that calls forth from others their noblest endeavors. Who has not had reason to look back in gratitude to the memory of an encounter with a person of such priceless gifts in love! Yet there is nothing dramatic about this love, and even the humblest may have the gift.

Love in its creative function may work on things and institutions as well as on persons. The historian Michelet fell in love with the archives in the public library, and, hearing them cry out to be brought back to life, decided to give them a resurrection in his writings. The youthful Charles Darwin, not yet a scientist, had such a tender regard for earthworms that he was unwilling to fix them on a fisherman's hook; and, when he became a man, his enlarged affection for these creatures helped him to write a famous treatise about them. A George Washington, not celebrated as a lover of women, and without any children of his own, can exercise a noble and austere love, and be known as the father of his country. A sculptor caressing a piece of marble, a greengrocer fondling his vegetables, a college president cherishing his plant and its people, can visit each object with an evocative power. For every gardener knows that, if you want to raise good vegetables or beautiful flowers, you must love them.

Love as a creator is not without its pains. A young husband sits by his young wife on her hospital bed, and for long hours they play gin rummy together. It seems like idle employment; but every few minutes there is a tension in her body, and an answering concern in his, as she feels the agony of a womb that wills to be delivered of its burden. At a critical moment she will be taken into another room, and, with the help of doctors and of nurses, the child will come. Later on there is the shared delight of holding in one's arms and of looking upon one's first offspring. After that there is much to come. Because of tensions between parent and child there will be new tensions between the parents. And there is everything of joy and of grief that mingles into infancy, adolescence, and at last what is supposed to be the status of a free, mature adult. But if, in all this, love is truly a creator, the joy will overbear the sorrow.

While the pessimists forget that love is a creator, the sentimentalists forget that love must also be a judge. This is to say that love is always accompanied by standards of excellence in conduct and in craftsmanship. Indeed there can be no escaping the imperative to make judgments of value. Herbert Spencer pointed out that even animals learn to distinguish between friend and foe, safety and danger, health and disease. When the Latin saying that there can be no disputing about questions of taste was cited to Nietzsche's Zarathustra, the answer came back, "On the contrary, all life is a dispute about taste and tasting." Love may not wash its hands of moral responsibility and seek to put off an awkward judgment onto others. This can only mean that those who do not love will make a loveless judgment.

What warrants us in making a judgment is not our own righteousness.[3] In *King Lear* it is argued that the judge and the jury may have as much guilt in their souls as does the criminal in court; but in *Measure for Measure* it is affirmed, in the Biblical manner, that each one must make his judgment when he is called upon to do so, and then be ready to be judged with the same judgment with which he has judged another. Often when we refrain from judgment, we allege that we do not want to hurt the feelings of others, but it can also be that we are cowards who do not wish to upset our own feelings. The important thing, the difficult thing, in passing judgment is to be free from pride and self-righteousness, and to blend force and firmness with humility and charity. It was because of the love that evades judgment that Spinoza as well as Nietzsche could declare that pity is debilitating. Prin-

ciple without compassion may be cruel, but compassion
without principle corrupts.

At the same time it will help individuals as well as
nations to remember that, in Reinhold Niebuhr's phrase,
we are but the executors of judgment. For there is only
one true Judge, and we can be only his instruments. As
he could use Assyria as the rod of his anger against Israel,
so can he, at any moment, make use of a less worthy
person to chastise one who is more worthy. There is, besides, a Last Judgment; for we do not have forever to
run our course. Nor is there any transmigration of souls
so that we can have another chance in another lifetime.
Nor should we deceive ourselves in this once-for-all lifetime because rewards or retributions are delayed beyond
our expectations. As Christian love reckons with reality,
so does it reckon not only with specific judgments but
also with the climactic judgment that must come to every
man.

Again, love must do its work as redeemer. Here the
critical confrontation is with an enemy who has done us
an injury, and the first thing we have to do is to forgive.
Reinhold Niebuhr says often that forgiveness is the most
difficult of all the Christian virtues for us to practice. Yet
the Scriptures tell us to forgive seventy times seven,
which, in effect, is to forgive forever. Of course there is a
sound reason in common sense why we should do so. It
would be impossible for others to live with us unless they
forgave us day in and day out for faults of which we are
quite unaware. Our forgiveness of others, therefore, is in
reciprocity for their continuing forgiveness of us. But
the deeper hurt that comes from a special injury is not so
easily overlooked. We are told that, if we want to merit
God's forgiveness, we had better show forgiveness to

others. It is not made clear whether forgiveness should always wait upon repentance. However, in the final agony of the cross, Jesus practiced a transcendent forgiveness when he prayed, "Father, forgive them for they know not what they do."[4]

Forgiveness and reconciliation are a part of redemption. So also is sacrifice when it is a vicarious atonement for the sins of others. The unique vision of an entire nation which, as the Suffering Servant of the Lord, should be a sacrifice for the sins of other nations is a vision of the prophet Isaiah for the Jewish people.[5] It is a vision which has had its fulfillments in history. In the New Testament Jesus comes as an individual person to take on himself the sins of mankind. While this ideal of love as sacrificially atoning may appear extravagant and theatrical in its pretensions, it is nevertheless a part of the business of living. There is no parent, no pastor, no public leader worthy of the name who has not shared in its ministries. Shakespeare had a clear vision of it when he wrote his first tragedy of *Romeo and Juliet*. While his chief concern was with a romantic love, he nevertheless understood that his story was a naturalistic paraphrase of the divine love. In the prologue he made plain his awareness that it was the death of the innocent lovers that healed the hatreds of the Montagues and the Capulets, and brought the two houses together in reconciliation.

If I were to amend Niebuhr's dictum, I should say that, while forgiveness may be against the grain of the hardness of the heart, it is the whole work of redemption which is most difficult to achieve. Love as creator or as judge flows from us more easily than does love as redeemer; for to play the redeemer is to pay a great price. So the Christian believes that there is but one Redeemer, whose grace works in us as mercy for our sins and also as power to do more than we could otherwise do. But our Redeemer and our Judge and our Creator are all one in the expression of God's love.

The Rewards of Love

But what shall it profit a man to love in this wise? The answer here will be strictly in terms of this world.

From a self-regarding point of view, one of the rewards of giving love is that we receive it in return. When love calls forth the response of love, it is one of the most wonderful experiences in life. Most of us need this response of love from others to nourish us in our capacity for giving love, for few of us have so saintly a disposition that we can take all our strength for loving in response solely to God's love for us. Yet we must beware of any kind of book-keeping by which we should keep accounts of so much love expended and of so much love received, and consider carefully how to invest our loving with the greatest likelihood of a profitable return to our private selves. The income and the outgo of love do not flow in such orderly channels, and if we are greedy for what we get we shall soon become powerless to give. But if we give with a generous heart, and are grieved when there is no response in love, we may yet rejoice in those many occasions when there is an unexpected harvest of gratitude and love and joy.

From an other-regarding point of view one of the chief rewards of love is to see its fruits in the life of another. In its simple, creative function, as evocative of hidden potentialities, love works its wonders every day. It does as much also when it serves as judge with firmness and with charity, or serves as redeemer with forgiveness and in sacrifice. Children who are blessed with good parents inevitably take for granted the services in love they receive, for they do not know a different situation. Often enough the gratitude and appreciation come after the giver is gone: so of a church for its pastor, after he has resigned; of a nation for its governor, after he is deposed; of a people for its leader, after he is slain and martyred. But such a one, if he has given love, has already seen some of its fruits in the time of his stewardship, and knows that there will be others in time to come. As it is written of this love, "there is no limit to its faith, its hope, and its endurance."[6]

The Christian realist, however, knows that love may have cross consequences. It may provoke only contempt, with an effort at exploitation. For a person of a tough and predatory disposition will think that all Christian lovers are ninnies who require to be used for what can be got out of them and then discarded as so much waste material. Indeed, if our loving is not fully informed with a Christian discipline, we may even invite such a response. It was for such a reason that Herbert Spencer wrote in some detail on the danger that unselfishness may breed and nourish selfishness in others. But if we love with a Christian love, it should be revealed in time that such love is not weakness, but is strength.

Another response to love can be hatred. He who gave the world the greatest love was rewarded also by hate. The early Christians were advised, "My brothers, do not be surprised if the world hates you."[7] Now it does not follow that, whenever others hate us, it is because we are such generous lovers. But the fact is that true love is a subversive: it works toward the breaking down of barriers and the overturning of kingdoms, and, as Jesus said, it may bring fire on earth and strife.[8] So there are those that hate it, as the children of darkness hate the light; and, when they discover an apostle of that love, they will seek to crucify him.

Hatred and contempt can be had, if necessary; but the hardest of all to reckon with is a complete indifference. There are many who simply do not wish to be bothered. This may be due, sometimes, to a thoughtlessness in our loving—because we are meddlesome, or officious, or exhibitionist, or imperialistic. But apart from that there are surely those who do not wish to be disturbed in their carnal complacencies, or provoked to a level of aspiration where either love or hate can have any meaning at all.

The chief reward of love, however, comes from the fact that love is the law of our being. Aristotle understood that the happiness of any creature depends on its being what it is meant to be. This is its power, its peace, and its joy. This is what is meant when we say that virtue is its own reward. So when the disciples thought that Jesus was hungry and urged him to eat, he replied, "It is meat and drink for me to do the will of him who sent me until I have finished his work."[9] So also Marcus Aurelius has written: "As a horse after a race, and a hunting dog when he hath hunted, and a bee when she hath made her honey, look not for applause and commendation; so neither doth that man that doth rightly understand his own nature when he hath done a good turn; but from one doth proceed to do another, even as the vine after she hath once borne fruit in her own proper season, is ready for another time."

So the reward of loving is that we are able to love again.

3

Love Against Lust

"I will lift up mine eyes unto the hills, from whence cometh my help."[1] This is the way we learned to read it in the King James Version of the Bible. In response to this, many of us have been inspired to descant on the majesty of the mountains as they reflect the majesty of God their creator. Then along came the Higher Criticism and punctured our ecstasies. We were informed there should be a period after "hills," and a question mark after "help," so that the correct reading would be, "I lift up my eyes to the hills. From whence does my help come?" To be sure, my help still comes from the Lord who made heaven and earth. But there is no sign of him on the hills, because that is where the heathen have their high places to celebrate pagan rituals.

A visitor to Corinth today can be grateful for the insights of the Higher Criticism. On the plain and by the water are the remnants of the old city and of the seaport, once the center of a thriving commercial activity. It must have been in the forum on the plain that Paul talked to the people. But if he lifted up his eyes to the hill towering above him, he saw on the crest the Temple of Aphrodite, with its one thousand temple prostitutes, and with its busy trade in the flesh, as it catered to the clients of the merchants with the big expense accounts. When Paul talked about love in Corinth, and later wrote about it so eloquently, he was confronting its two most palpable enemies: hatred and lust.

As for the uses of lust in that day, they were a part of the ethical establishment. Curiously enough, what we like to call the New Morality was in that time the Old Morality. It was Saint Paul who preached the New Morality—of love.

THE CYCLE OF LOVE AND OF LUST

If anyone is enamored, like Spengler and like the entire Sinico-Hindu-Hellenic tradition, with the idea of a cyclical pattern in history, he can find abundant evidence for it in the record of our sexual folkways. There seems to be a perpetual swing of the pendulum, as Schopenhauer would have it, from desire frustrated to desire satisfied, from restraint and austerity to lust, license, and disgust, and then back again. Only, there is no telling how long a given cycle shall endure, or under what peculiar circumstances each of its phases shall emerge and then submerge.

In any case there is nothing really new about the so-called new morality in sex today. The revolt against moral restraints in this area of activity is as old as the problem of the first Israelite families that settled in Canaan and had to guard their offspring against the enticements of the fertility cults, as old as the breakdown of Roman sexual morality coincident with the decline and fall of the Roman Empire, as old as the flamboyant dispersion of all sexual restraints in the England of the Restoration which succeeded the rule of Cromwell and the Puritans.

There is a sense in which the cycle is new in the United States of America, because this is a very young country, and because heretofore the prevailing morality has been on the side of restraint. The present revolt, however, is not the work of any members of a current younger generation. Actually it began with their grandparents. Its inception can be dated with precision from the conclusion of World War I. It was then that the first efforts to disrupt Puritan morality began to show point and power. Since then we have gradually developed a situation which can best be described as sex on the loose. It is characterized by the discarding of many historic controls, by more flagrant if not more widespread indulgence in premarital sexual intercourse, by more extramarital pregnancies in so-called good families, by earlier forced marriages, and by resort to adoption agencies beyond the capacity of those agencies to take care of the unwanted babies. Among the more emancipated spirits this complex of activities is generally referred to as the "new freedom."

Actually in the history of sexual folkways there is only one innovation of any significance—the emancipation of women. The essential is the recognition that women, too, are human beings, are persons. It happens that, in American history, this made for a special burst of activity right after the First World War, at the same time as the change in sexual morality. Women suddenly had the right to vote, and reached out to establish other equalities—legal, political, economic, educational, vocational, spiritual, sexual. In the first phase of this movement, the emancipated woman asserted her right to be and to do anything that a man might be and do.

But after fifty years of exploiting such liberties, there is evidence that women are beginning to ask, not "What does a man do that I want to do, too?" but "What do I want to do that is true to my nature as a woman?" It is still the case that women, not men, bear the babies; that girls talk more of love, while boys talk more of sex; and recent polls on college campuses indicate that more than half as many women as men hold to chastity before marriage. Is it possible that the finally emancipated woman is turning conservative on sex? Whose then will be the "new morality"?

SEX, LOVE, AND COMMON SENSE

There is an ethics of sexual morality within the context of love that is as age-old and as widespread as common sense. There are five guiding principles to its code:

1. *Either you control sex, or sex controls you.* Needed right now are bigger and better inhibitions. Let no one be afraid to speak to young people today in this manner. It is a message they have not heard in a quarter of a century, and it will come to them with all the charm of novelty. Currently they have a respectful awareness that they must curb their appetites for food, drink, and tobacco. This message comes to them with all the authority of science, of the federal government, and of the beauty parlor. Surely there is something ludicrous in the notion that, while liquor, cigarettes, and ice cream must be put under the most strict controls, sex, on the other hand, is something to which you may help yourself when, as, and if you please.

Personal responsibility in such a matter cannot be abdicated because of the temptations of the environment, or because of dependence on the pill. Almost any kind of environment, with or without overt solicitation of our sexual appetites, can provide the temptations. And while there may be an infallible pill, there is no infallible patient. It is commonplace that married couples often do not get babies when they want them, and do get babies when they do not want them. As for the really young people today, the tragedy is that they are losing control of their lives. They are having babies when they don't want them; they are getting married before they really want to; and they are taking jobs before they are prepared to earn a living. Is this the "new freedom"?

2. *Sexual compatibility is not the irreducible essential in a happy marriage.* This statement will scandalize the sentimentalists of sex, but let us look at the facts. Theoretically there are four possible combinations: happiness with sexual compatibility, or without it; unhappiness with sexual compatibility, or without it. Only two of these cases supply critical evidence.

Can people be sexually compatible, and still develop an unhappy marriage? Obviously so. The fact is that the ordinary, normal person is capable of having physically satisfactory sexual relations with some millions of persons of the opposite sex. The difficulty arises when he discovers that this is the only satisfactory relationship he has. When that discovery is made, then boredom and ennui set in, and the sexual relationship itself begins to degenerate.

Can people be sexually incompatible and still have a happy marriage? This varies with the kind and degree of incompatibility. The important thing is whether the other factors in a happy marriage are present or absent. Any marriage counselor knows that there are happily married couples whose experience of the usual consummation of sexual intercourse is limited or infrequent. In such circumstances it may still be possible to have children, to create a home, to develop significant fellowship with one another.

If premarital experiments in sexual compatibility are misleading, it is because the participants tend to make an absolute out of the sexual relationship. But happiness in marriage depends on a love and a loyalty which can stand the long-range test for better or for worse, for richer or for poorer, in sickness and in health. The important thing is not our ability to go to bed with someone, but our ability to get out of bed and face the workaday world with the loved one.

3. *Sex is for human beings.*   To be sure, it is also for vegetables and for animals, as Aristotle knew. And the idyllic South Sea Islander of the poet and of the cultural anthropologist is just as human as we are. But most of us do not live in any such simplistic paradise. Our common humanity endows us with the capacity for love and for intelligence, and for free and responsible decision. And our special humanity places us in a complex culture, where we have high-strung nerves, an educated intellect, and sophisticated senses and emotions. Each of us, as he strives for moral excellence, must do it according to the order and degree of his own humanity.

Perhaps we can get some help here from a famous marriage counselor:

Dear Abby: Three months ago I met a pretty nurse and we have been going together ever since. She has lived with another man for the past two years in an intimate, but unexciting (she claims) relationship. She is now dividing her time between us. She says she loves me, but she continues to live with this man. She says it would be impractical for her to move out.

I am very fond of her and want her to devote herself completely to me. Would it be advisable for me to insist on her total loyalty and risk losing her? Or should I knowingly share her and leave things as they are? Please ignore the question of morality and answer me frankly.

                                          IN DOUBT.

Dear IN DOUBT: One who is concerned with HUMAN relations cannot "ignore the question of morality." Since morality is what sets us apart from the beasts, and you choose to ignore it, I suggest you direct your inquiry to a veterinarian.

The crisp common sense of Abigail Van Buren is often an offense to the professional psychologist. At this point, however, she is supported by the authority of Immanuel Kant and of Charles Darwin. Alfred Kinsey or Walt Whitman may seek to entice us with a romantic primitivism to go back and live with the animals. But we must decide, when we take our sex, whether we do it as pigs or as people.

4. *Sex is social.* In our culture sexual relations have their origin in the free choice and consent of individuals. But the outcome is always social. That is why there is no society whatsoever, from the most primitive to the most complex, that does not regulate sexual conduct by its folkways. This is true even with what may look to us like primitive patterns of promiscuity—which, however, are socially defined and circumscribed in the most careful manner. In the modern world the most severely "Puritan"

constraints on sex are exercised not in any capitalist democracy but in Communist China. Obviously sex has a
social outcome that is biological in the form of babies;
but it also has social outcomes that are vocational, economic, civil, political, aesthetic, and religious. For this
reason, whether we inhabit More's *Utopia* or B. F. Skin-
ner's *Walden II*, or live in the world of Orwell's *1984* or
Huxley's *Ape and Essence*, the rulers see to it that sex is
made subservient to ends of which they approve.

The great delusion here—especially pronounced among
adolescents of all ages—is the delusion that, in sexual affairs, each of us can play the isolated individual. Adeline
Daley has written a comical column on "Sex and the
P.T.A. Den-Mother." Here she asks how you can manage
a big family of children—get them off to school and the
husband off to work each day, clean the house, buy the
groceries, cook the meals, serve on assorted committees,
act as chauffeur for assorted good causes—and still be
ready in the evening to play the role of the love goddess
that is called for in the manuals of marital eroticism. The
point is that the final test of love is social. Love does not
know itself as love until it has entered into a community
with groceries, taxes, property, babies, wages, and civic
and religious responsibilities. Moreover, it is precisely this
social experience that makes love a truly individual affair.
As Thielicke observes, "Not uniqueness establishes marriage, but marriage establishes uniqueness."

5. *Sex is for persons.* The ultimate evil is when sex is
depersonalized. Being a person implies the full social context, and also involves the genuine emotion of love. Yet
people will still argue that sex can be cut off from its
organic relationship to the affections and to the social

order, and be taken in isolation by itself. Of course it can. So can you cut off a hand, or an arm, or a head, and take it by itself. But what happens to the separated organ, and what happens to the dismembered person? If someone practicing such a dismemberment of sex argues, "What I'm doing can't harm anyone else," then the answer is clear: "It will not at once harm anyone but you—by gradually converting you into a selfish sensualist incapable of loyalty and affection for another."

In Rostand's *Last Night of Don Juan,* the devil, in the guise of a puppeteer, comes to pick up the great lover at the moment of his death. Don Juan pleads for more time; argues that he was always in love with his women; asks that his mistresses be brought back to testify for him. As they go by in parade, each holds a mask to her face. He steps up eagerly, to identify one and then the other: "Henriette!—Louise!—Jeanne-Marie!" In every instance there is the tinkling laughter of mockery, as the mask is withdrawn to show the mistake in identity, while the woman bows ironically and goes on her way. This Don Juan, who thought he knew all about women, had never known a woman as a person. He had long ago ceased to be a person himself. And he had never really been in love with anyone but himself and his own narcistic sensations. So the devil takes Don Juan to his reward, with the decree that one who has made a puppet of himself in this life must be forever hereafter a puppet in hell.

And that surely is the heart of the matter. Sex must be a part of the self as a person. Like any other healthy appetite it needs regulation and control. Nor shall we get the most out of it, or out of ourselves, unless we mingle it with those elements that are moral and spiritual and social and call forth the highest in our humanity.

This takes us finally past a commonsense code of sexual morality to one principle of uncommon sense. *Romantic love requires the vision and the discipline of the Christian faith if it is to realize the best.* What is meant here by romantic love is the ardent attachment of a man and a woman to each other. What it requires of the Christian vision is the capacity to see the other person as a child of God for whom Christ died, even when the evidence of the immediate does not appear to support such a vision. What it requires of the Christian discipline is the capacity to rise to a level of love which, in a moment of crisis, can transcend liking, respect, mutuality, and reciprocity. For it is precisely in the relationship of marriage, where so much of what is good and of what is evil in each of us is shared so intimately, that we face the severest tests in affection. It is just here that there can be the terrible moment when respect and mutuality seem to break down, and when only a religious imperative can have the power to carry us through. And it is only when we have passed through that ordeal that we can move on to a love that is infinitely richer than the simple romantic attachment with which we began. It is not only my country, it is also my family that needs to be embraced "under God."

THE NEW MORALITY AND THE OLD

The ironical aspect of discussions about sexual morality in America today is that those who call themselves situationists in ethics are so out-of-date in their analysis of the situation. For the tyranny of a so-called "Puritan ethic" has been going, or gone, for almost half a century. The forces today that are "anti-sex" are to be found in the camp of those who pretend to be the liberators of sex.

And in this camp what a strange assortment do we find of situational sexperts.

There are, for instance, the rationalists. These believe that by some device of reason or of science we can contain human passion and caprice. Again, there are the non-directive libertarians. One of them, a medical doctor, urges tenth- and twelfth-graders to observe "sexual responsibility. Don't enter premarital sex lightly. Enter it after deep and searching thought . . . Premarital sex should be entered into as a faithful episode. You choose your mate carefully and remain faithful at the time." Another one, a doctor of divinity, also feels that we should move "forward" in sexual morality, while exercising a "responsible liberty" and "walking in the Spirit" and "doing all things to the glory of God." But how "deep and searching" is one's thought in such circumstances? What sort of faithfulness is it that is confined to an "episode"? And how "responsible" are we being when we attribute an action from impulse to the agency of the Holy Ghost? Surely this sort of talk is the last gasp of a permissive Pelagianism in pedagogy.

There are also the idolaters and the iconoclasts. The one group says that Sex Is Everything. In this tradition belong Schopenhauer, Freud, Shaw, Havelock Ellis, Walt Whitman. Curiously enough, the first of these hated sex; the second had a very mild sex drive; the third and the fifth were total abstainers; and the fourth was impotent during the better part of his career. In the second group are those who say that Sex Is Nothing at All. Their disposition is to belittle the importance of the sexual act, and to view it with the most casual concern; so that, whether we encounter it in harlotry or in the home, it is just to be taken as so much good clean fun, but not to be seen as an enterprise that has any significant impact upon the whole personality. Both the idolaters, as they inflate sex out of all proportion, and the iconoclasts, as they attenuate sex into a trifle, are the real forces of an anti-sex campaign in our culture.

Perhaps the best way to understand the situation in which we find ourselves today is to look at an entirely different situation. William Shakespeare was not known to be an enemy of sex. The Renaissance-Elizabethan world in which he lived was not a Puritan's world. The popular audience to which he directed his plays did not suffer from sexual inhibitions. Yet in Act IV, scene 3, of *Macbeth*, when Prince Malcolm wants to prove his fitness to succeed to the throne in the place of the tyrant, he declares, "I am yet Unknown to woman." Here we have a man who is a soldier, who must lead his troops into battle, and then be crowned a king, publicly boasting that he is still a virgin. An Elizabethan audience took this with quiet approval. One can imagine the titters, the sniggers, the derisive laughter that would greet a modern hero in a similar situation today. Indeed, if the modern hero were still chaste in his passions, would he dare to confess it? Would he not, rather, boast with lies about his conquests of women?

All of this helps to define the situation in which we find ourselves at the moment. If we are fatalists about the cycles of history, then we shall acquiesce in the way things are, be willing conformists to the fashion of the times, and school ourselves as the docile puppets of blind circumstance. But if we really care for a responsible freedom, perhaps the time has come to let out a prolonged rebel yell. It is time to rebel against what proclaims itself as the New Establishment in sexual conduct. It is time to rebel against lust and disgust in behalf of sex and love. And whatever may be the new or the old of the matter, we may be sure, with Saint Paul, that the only morality in which sex can come to significant fulfillment is the morality of love.

4

Love Against Violence

As love is opposed to lust, so is love opposed to hate. Lust is a corruption of the flesh; hate is a corruption of the spirit. Thus Satan is depicted as consumed by an unremitting hatred, for God, for men, and for the whole order of creation. Hatred is unable to create; it can only destroy. But it destroys itself as much as it destroys another. So the apostle warns the Galatians, "If you go on fighting one another, tooth and nail, all you can expect is mutual destruction."[1] The outward show of hate is violence. For violence is the use of force to destroy.

The Bloody City

The American people in much of their history have been a people of violence. In part this is our heritage from the frontier, with its battle against the wilderness and the Indians, with its absence of police and of courts, and with its vigilantes for summary justice. It extends through the Ku Klux Klan, the Industrial Workers of the World, the struggle of labor for its rights, and assorted populist movements. It flourishes especially under the pampering permissiveness of an affluent society, in which we understand neither the patience required to work out a thing nor the price to be paid for a thing, and expect to achieve any end by the device of the timely tantrum. So it is that we build ourselves a City of Blood.

The hoodlums of hatred are the inhabitants of this City of Destruction. Some are in high places, some are in low; some are white, some black. In the language of this City there is a new definition of old terms. A conservative is anyone who will not resort to violence to gain his ends. It does not matter, then, if radicals come from the right or from the left; they are blood brothers in a passion to wreck and to ruin. Again, a liberal is anyone who is easily intimidated by violence, and, in his desire to be sweetly reasonable, will always give way to the most violent. So the liberal is held in contempt by the bully-boys who bear rule in the City of Destruction. The liberal is the hysteric who tremulously anticipates riot before it occurs, celebrates it while it takes place, justifies it after it is over. The liberal is the masochist, rejoicing in his guilty conscience, and eagerly prostrating himself before the whips in the hands of the flagellators.

In this City of Blood the sensation-mongers are those who control the radio, the press, and television. The theater of sadomasochism provides the formula for determining what the public may want. Herewith, as reported by Terence O'Flaherty, is a sample of soap opera for domestic consumption:

Susan became pregnant last season and decided to marry David, put the baby up for adoption and get a divorce so David could marry her best friend Julie whom he really loved. But after the baby was born Susan decided against the divorce, and one day while David played with the child he accidentally dropped him and he died. Susan killed

David but was acquitted. Then David's mother shot Susan making her an invalid for life. Now Julie, who is pregnant with David's baby, is out to kill Susan.

This sort of soap opera is for the unenlightened house-wife. The intelligentsia delight in the same sort of fare, but want it spiced with tart symbolism from psychology and sociology.

In this City there is also a politics of sadomasochism. It is a politics which believes in the fist, the club, the bomb, the bullet, and which practices routine assassination. In one community some black children are murdered in the church where they worship. In another a young president of the republic is slain. In another a great emancipator of men is shot down. In still another the younger brother of the young president is assassinated. Cry, "Woe to the bloody city! . . Woe to the bloody city of Birmingham! . . Woe to the bloody city of Dallas! . . Woe to the bloody city of Memphis! . . Woe to the bloody city of Los Angeles! . . Behold, the blood of our brothers and sisters cries out to us from the ground . . . Woe to the bloody city which is the United States of America!"[2]

WHAT VIOLENCE IS

If violence generically is the use of force for purely destructive ends, it yet needs to be understood in more precise detail. Three definitions are required to cover what goes on today.

The first and classical definition of violence is that it is injury to persons or to property. In this sense we speak of mob violence and of the violence of war. When nonviolent resistance was developed as an art by Gandhi and then adopted by Martin Luther King, it abjured this primary form of violence. And it added moral authority to itself in that the resisters were willing, if need be, to suffer violence from others while holding themselves under the strict discipline of love.

There is a second definition of violence, however, which belongs to a more tough and realistic tradition. Here violence is the use of force in excess of or apart from the end to be achieved. To be sure, some kind of force is necessary to achieve any end. Violence, then, has to do with the relationship of the means to the end. To the realist the use of excess or of misdirected energies is a waste of powers; and it may bring about collateral consequences that will bury the end-in-view.

So every ineffectual use of force becomes an act of violence, whether the use is by a majority or by a minority, by those in the right or by those in the wrong. For a modern army the practice of rape and of pillage is militarily outrageous. Such excesses destroy military discipline, expose the army to the enemy, make more difficult the later problem of pacification. For an oppressed minority the resort to arson and to riot in its own neighborhood does no good. So the Reverend Andrew J. Young urges that the race riots of the summer of 1967 were wasteful, in that it was the Negroes themselves who suffered the most injury to persons and to property, and in that the net consequence was to promote reaction, not progress. Power is a means which must come under the discipline of the end.

There is a third meaning of violence, which may be the fundamental one. It has to do with the nature of the self. From Aristotle to Dewey we have been taught that the self *is* its interests and activities. This is true of any private person. It is equally true of any public person, which in law is a way of designating a corporation. Essential violence, then, is anything that obstructs the legitimate functioning of the activities of a person. This is the kind of violence which is most radically resented. It can be perpetrated, moreover, without resort to either the first or the second kind of violence.

If I am a man who loves his family, and you obstruct my fellowship with wife and children, you do me violence. If I am a teacher, or a preacher, and you keep me from books, and deny me access to a classroom or to a congregation, you give me a mortal wound. So also for an institution—whether a university, or a draft board, a grocery store, a church, a courthouse, or a country club—if it is blocked in the activities which constitute its essential functions, it undergoes an intolerable violence.

VIOLENCE IN OUR TIME

It is this last definition which gives meaning to what is called systemic violence, or implicit violence. This is the built-in violence of social institutions and customs so far as they deny to any human being his normal right to function as a human being.

There is no reason to believe that every member of the lowest stratum of society in a democracy is the victim of such violence. But it is clear that our Afro-Americans long have been and still are the victims of implicit violence in American culture. It is natural, too, that they should entertain feelings of violence in resentment of the violence imposed upon them. But it does not follow that implicit violence is best healed by resort to explicit violence. As for the white part of the community, it has an obligation to render justice, as the black part of the community has an obligation to strike for justice. It should be understood, moreover, that the restitution of rights is in no sense a bestowal of privileges. A right is that to which any man in civil society is entitled; and, when the right is restored, then society owes not only the principal but some payment of interest for the disabilities suffered during the period of wrongful withholding.

As for explicit violence in the United States, it is overwhelmingly a youth phenomenon. It is only a small fraction of our youth—whether of the low-minded or criminal sort, or of the high-minded and idealistic sort—that resorts to violence. Also, white youth got into the act long before it was taken up by black youth. Rioting by white youth at house parties, or at beach resorts, or at jazz festivals, or in the rape of a village by a gang of motorcyclists, set the tone for this sort of thing before the urban riots conducted by Negro young people took place.

But contrary to the teaching of the sentimentalists, such rioting is not the consequence of intolerable abuses. It is more likely to be the consequence of excessive liberties. It is the product of privilege and of affluence operating against a background of broken morale. The disintegration of authority in the Negro home exists in equal measure in the white home. So it is the Negro youth, not the Negro oldsters, who riot in the cities; they riot in the North, not in the South; and they riot now that they begin to get their rights rather than to lose them. Also the white youth who riot come from homes of comfort, leisure, and relative affluence. In brief, American youth resort to riot when they know they can get away with it.

A third area for violence is war. Obviously war is always involved in violence under the first and third definitions. While this writing is in no sense a treatise on social ethics, we may at least raise a question, with reference to the realistic definition of violence as a relationship between means and ends in the use of force, and ask when a war is a violent one in the militarily invidious sense. The greatest loss of life in American history was in the Civil War. It was a war of brother against brother. It was motivated in the South by the love of liberty, and in the North by the love of the Union and a love of the black man. It was won for the North under General Grant, who was known as "the butcher" because of the terrible loss of life that took place in his victories. Would Abraham Lincoln have been a more Christian president if he had not called upon this "butcher" to win his war?

Eighty years later men of reason would be proving that the Civil War was not an historical necessity, while at the same time other men of reason were preparing the devices that would enable us to drop an atom bomb on Hiroshima. Yet this destruction by an atom bomb did not bring so much suffering to the Japanese as did the fire-bombing of Tokyo. How then do we apply Grotius' rules of moderation in the conduct of a just war?

WHEN THE NONVIOLENT TURN TO VIOLENCE

Unhappily it is the case that often those who begin with love and sweet reasonableness will later turn to violence. Under what circumstances does this occur?

When idealists become impatient—when perfectionism is wed to instantism—we get violence. There is a memorandum, from over one hundred years ago, from Blanqui to Proudhon, with the warning that the doctrines of a rational anarchism, if they should touch the breasts of

susceptible persons, might arouse turbulent passions. In
the United States in the 1920's liberals took up a crusade
in defense of two noble anarchists, Sacco and Vanzetti;
but later scrutinies of their case in *Commentary* and in
The Antioch Review would indicate that at least one of
them succumbed to the temptation to bring in the Kingdom of Heaven by violence.[3] In recent years, also, we
have seen a Student Nonviolent Coordinating Committee
lose both its students and its discipline of nonviolence.
Indeed, every utopian is tempted to believe that, by a
sudden act of destruction, he should be enabled at once
to enter paradise.

When idealists are disillusioned, they may resort to violence. After all, the sentimentalist and the cynic are two
sides of the same person. The sentimentalist expects to
effect all changes by the appeal to right reason and to
goodwill; but, when these facile devices fail him, he turns
bitter and savage. This is already illustrated in the evolution of the hippies. What was once a community of mutual
trust and of easy camaraderie degenerates, before our
eyes, into an uneasy, milling mob, with whom obscenities,
switchblades, and sudden assault have taken over from
flower-power. In brief, the hippies of yesterday are the
hoodlums of today.

When idealists are played for suckers by the tough
guys, then violence prevails. A fifteen-year veteran of the
peace movement resigns from an important office because
the movement has been infiltrated by those who wish to
exploit peace for strife. A political party calling itself the
Peace and Freedom Party sells out to a group of militants
whose chief action is to disturb the peace and to deny
civil freedoms to anyone in disagreement with them. At
a state college a gang of students and nonstudents threat-

ens the tenure of the college president by acts of violence; but, when he is impeached for not resisting violence, they threaten more violence in order to keep in office the man who permitted their violence. So it is that the nonviolent become the tools of the violent.

In the Scriptures we are told to combine the innocence of the dove with the wisdom of the serpent.[4] So a Christian should be schooled in the wisdom of this world, even though the faith by which he finally lives is but foolishness to that same wisdom.[5] We live in a world in which various kinds of force—political, economic, military, technological—are in constant use; and we are not excused by our idealism for being ignorant of these other forces, even though we may believe that love is the greatest of all forces. In any case it is outrageous that those who profess love should be the first to fawn upon those who most profess violence.

THE FRUITS OF VIOLENCE

As violence is the fruit of hatred, so does violence have its own fruits. The first of these is terror and intimidation. In the case of the implicit violence of the white against the black, whether with a white majority in the United States or with a white minority in South Africa, the impact of such systemic violence against the black man is to destroy his dignity, his humanity, his selfhood. In the case of explicit violence, whether practiced by black youth in urban ghettos or practiced by white (and sometimes black) youth on college campuses, we have the example of the terrorizing of a majority by a minority. The larger number of black people in the United States have no expectation that their basic problems will be solved by acts of violence, and the overwhelming majority of students on our college campuses are opposed to the violent disruption of their academic liberties. Nevertheless, when a peace-loving people sees that even those in positions of authority are intimidated by acts of violence, then the many will succumb to the terrorism of the few.

When violence is allowed to run its full course, the final outcome can only be tyranny and dictatorship. Because a society cannot long abide a condition of anarchy and licentiousness. At this point it matters little whether the dictatorship comes from the left or from the right, whether it speaks eloquently of conserving the great values of the past, or provides fine talk about the illusory liberties of a participatory people's democracy. A dictatorship is the fitting reward of those who do not know how to exercise power with wisdom and with justice, and to govern themselves under the rule of law, of intelligence, and of love. And a dictator, in a black shirt or in a red shirt, is one who destroys all human freedoms.

While we associate violence chiefly with war, we should understand that there is a difference between a disciplined army and an army that practices a wanton violence. It is curious, too, that hatred is an emotion less frequent with fighting men than with civilians. Having served on an attack transport in World War II, I can testify that I knew only one instance, among the men we carried from the staging area to the scene of assault, of a soldier consumed by a feeling of hatred for the enemy; and I remember this instance because it was so notable an exception. Indeed, in wartime hatred would seem to be a luxury of the civilian population. In a time of peace and of prosperity, moreover, it must be a shocking experience to any professional soldier to observe the luxuriant hatreds that seethe in the breasts of self-righteous civilians and spill over into passionate acts of violence.

The reason why soldiers do not hate is that they soon learn that hatred is an inefficient emotion. When we are dealing with affairs of life and of death, we cannot afford such dangerously foolish feelings. Hatred is never an effective instrument of warfare. It may occasionally provoke men to fight; it will never enable them to win a fight. For the final fruit of the violence which is the fruit of hatred is that it destroys itself. Hatred stupefies the intellect; it enlarges the imagination with lunatic visions; it shrivels and constricts our energies; it paralyzes our powers. Hatred at last hurts only the hater. Even in pure prudence no soldier of Christ dare let this poison come pouring into his veins.

The Unarmed Prophet

If we love our enemy, it does not mean that we cease to fight him, or to fight the thing for which he stands.[6] For loving can be another way of fighting. So Spinoza wrote, "Hatred is increased by reciprocal hatred, and, on the other hand, can be destroyed by love." And Martin Luther King wrote: "Returning hate for hate multiplies hate, adding deeper darkness to a night already devoid of stars. Darkness cannot drive out darkness; only light can do that." Again: "Love is the only force capable of transforming an enemy into a friend . . . Love transforms with redemptive power." Yet, realizing perhaps that what love can do it does not always manage to do, and that love itself can know defeat, he urges as the ultimate reason for loving our enemies the Scriptural injunction, "that ye may be the children of your Father which is in heaven."[7]

The particular strategy of nonviolent resistance, as first developed by Mahatma Gandhi and then elaborated by Martin Luther King, has already demonstrated its capacity to yield tremendous results in the common good. As a social strategy, however, it is most effective when two conditions obtain. The group that is putting up the resistance must be under the discipline of a great religious tradition that enables it to endure the rigors and the sacrifices of such an ordeal. Again, the power that is being resisted must be obliged to acknowledge the moral superiority of those who resist, until there is a gradual erosion of the authority of the oppressor. In other circumstances, in combating a ruthless totalitarian tyranny, such a strategy might be of no avail, and the Christian might feel obliged to resort to more peremptory modes of persuasion.

Nevertheless, even if we supplement the weapons of the spirit with the arms of the flesh, we are called upon to decide where lies our final confidence. Machiavelli, after considering the alternatives, wrote, "Hence it is that all armed prophets have conquered, and the unarmed ones have been destroyed." Martin Luther King wrote: "In a world depending on force, coercive tyranny, and bloody violence, you are challenged to follow the way of love. You will then discover that unarmed love is the most powerful force in the world." True it is that a Gandhi and a King are assassinated, even as our Lord was crucified. But has any of these been truly destroyed? Are we at last followers of the armed or of the unarmed prophet? May we believe with King that "unarmed love is the most powerful force in the world"?

In any case each one of us has this choice to make: to love or to hate, to create or to destroy. This is the first choice to be made, though it is not the final one. There are countless other decisions to be encompassed—of principle, of policy, of strategy, of tactics. It is not true that if only we should all love one another, then all our problems would be solved. Yet at the beginning we should know how lies the set of our minds and where is the source of our strength. Are we turned toward love, or are we turned toward hate? If we are turned toward love, then we are aligned with a power which is neither a black power nor a white power, nor a brown power nor a yellow, but only a human power, and a divine.

5

Love Against Anarchy

As love is opposed to lust and to violence, so is love opposed to anarchy. In the thinking of Saint Paul, Christian love is especially opposed to the sort of anarchy perpetrated in the name of some other sort of love or even in the name of the Holy Spirit. So it is that, at the conclusion of his critical discussion of the matter in I Corinthians, chapters 12 to 14, he urges, "Let all be done decently and in order."[1]

Today the principle of anarchy is enunciated again in various forms of what may be called a no-rules ethic. It derives from an existential ardor for an absolute freedom which is unconstrained by molds, patterns, or codes. It assures us that we are all the victims of an Establishment, or a System, or a Power Structure, and that now the time has come to strike a blow for liberty. But no matter how or where we live—even with Robinson Crusoe on his island—there is some kind of Establishment, or Power Structure. The only real choice is between an Establishment that is monolithic and inescapable, or a Structure of Powers that is plural, overlapping, and flexible in its functions. In either instance we may be sure of one thing: the system in which we find ourselves will have its rules of the game.

Bertrand Russell, whose autobiography hardly exhibits him as a model of propriety, makes this interesting observation about a certain Quaker lady who boasted of her disrespect for the ten commandments:

> I do not know whether any Quakers remain who take the doctrine of the guidance of the Holy Spirit so seriously as to have no respect for the Ten Commandments. Certainly I have not met any in recent years. It must not, of course, be supposed that the virtuous people who had this attitude ever, in fact, infringed any of the Commandments; the Holy Spirit saw to it that this should not occur. Outside the ranks of the Quakers, similar doctrines sometimes have more questionable consequences. I remember an account written by my mother-in-law of various cranks that she had known, in which there was one chapter entitled "Divine Guidance." On reading the chapter, one discovered that this was a synonym for fornication.

In brief, you can appear to hold in contempt the rules of the game provided you have been nurtured in the strict discipline of a good Quaker.

Nevertheless there is a distinguished English divine who preaches the doctrine that reality is a Heraclitean flux but without any Heraclitean logos to give order to the flux. He tells us that we should "embrace the relativities" of life and not be afraid of them. He also assures us that "God is in the rapids as much as in the rocks." Now it may be wrong to subject these exciting utterances to a literalistic scrutiny; but, granted that we always have to do with relativities and rocks and rapids, it is not clear to me that our chief business is to embrace any one of them so much as to cope with them in a constructive manner. Certainly to the swimmer or to the boatman there is both peril and promise in either the rocks or the rapids, in the stabilities of the shore or in the relativities of the river. I wish only to argue for a few principles of navigation.

There is also a distinguished American authority on the sexual behavior of college undergraduates, who is equally fascinated by a no-rules ethic. He urges that, while it is hazardous to drive automobiles, and many lives are lost each year in that venture, we still do not forbid the use of that vehicle. Likewise our young people must accept the risks that go with the sexual adventure. When I hear such counsels I am reminded of a certain foreign country where I had to drive a couple of hundred miles on a busy holiday weekend toward a popular seacoast resort, and was at first surprised and gradually terrified to observe the number of recently wrecked automobiles by the side of the road. Later on I learned that this state required no examination nor licensing of anyone who wished to handle an automobile, so that whoever had an inclination to ride at any time had only to jump into a car and take off. Certainly the comparison of the hazards of the automobile with the hazards of sex is an admirable one. But before we begin to play with such high-powered engines, why not first of all a little driver-training?

It is interesting that the great skeptic, David Hume, who was able to doubt God, the self, the soul, and the law of causality, had no doubts whatsoever about the importance of rules in ethics. At one place in his *Enquiry Concerning the Principles of Morals* he examines such questionable activities as piracy and highway robbery, drinking to the point of debauchery, immoral gallantry, and societies for gambling, and finds that, even in such circumstances, we learn "the necessity of rules, wherever men have intercourse with each other." One wonders what this skeptic would say in an encounter with theologians who believe they can dispense with rules because they have the guidance of the Holy Ghost, or a heart full of love, or because all they need is faith and the facts. Surely even when Saint Paul speaks of our having in us the "mind of Christ,"[2] that expression has meaning only because we have all the Gospels and the epistles, the Sermon on the Mount, and the endless rabbinical injunctions of the apostle himself to tell us what is in that "mind of Christ."

When we speak of a moral law, we are talking in terms of the widest and most inclusive generality. There will be more about this presently. When we speak of moral principles, we are already in the realm of diversity, but there is still great breadth of application. The principles enunciated under "Sex, Love, and Common Sense" are illustrative. When we talk about rules, we are dealing with what is local, specific, and, by agreement, subject to change. Nevertheless, we can have standards which are rules for rules. These are normative before they are descriptive. If in what follows I seem to mix rules with principles, that is because the distinction between them is not always clear, and often what appears to be a local rule turns out to be a universal principle.

RULES FOR RULES

1. *Rules are minimal, not maximal.* When the rich young ruler consults Jesus about what to do to inherit eternal life, he is told to "keep the commandments." When these are enumerated for his benefit, he is able to reply, "All these things have I kept from my youth up: what lack

I yet?" Jesus then tells him that if he wants to be "perfect," he must sell all that he has, give to the poor, and then come and follow Jesus. But the young man "went away sorrowful: for he had great possessions." In this instance Jesus is not rejecting the commandments. He is simply indicating that we have to go beyond them. The critical test for the rich young ruler lies in his possessions, because that is where lies the god of his idolatry.[3]

So often these days we have it announced to us, as though in a sudden revelation of a revolutionary truth, that obeying all the ten commandments will not make a man a good Christian. Of course it will not. Nor will it make a man a good Jew. The ten commandments are the least common denominator of a decent morality. Because they are inadequate to make us "perfect," it does not follow that we can ignore them or break them at will. What kind of society would it be in which men should steal, kill, commit adultery, bear false witness, dishonor their parents, and covet their neighbors' wives and property, and do so with complete abandon? And what kind of society would it be in which their chief priests should assure these men that such peccadilloes have no relevance to the weightier matters of the law?

The rules simply define the least we can do. But we do not achieve the most by holding in contempt the least. And if the least is all that we can manage in an affair, then we should be glad of that much. As a boy in China I learned to play soccer and cricket, according to the custom of the English which prevailed in sports in that country at that time. When I came to school in the United States I was embarrassed to find myself quite inept at baseball: I could neither throw a ball nor bat one with any skill. During my years as a graduate student, however,

I became a counselor in a boys' camp where one of my
duties was to coach the baseball team in our unit. With a
little study I undertook to learn the rules of the game, and
also some of the rules of strategy according to which one
makes use of a certain play or of a certain player at a
propitious time. The result was that the teams in our unit
won two different championships. I supplied the rules
and the discipline; the boys added the something extra
which made them "perfect." I could not be "perfect" myself, but I was happy to be able to contribute the mini-
mum necessary to an enterprise in which perfection might
be achieved by others.

2. *Rules are absolutes.*   At any rate, rules are meant to
be absolutes; although, due to accident or to inadvertence,
the absolute may not always be achieved. In any case,
the ethics of the golden mean is not supposed to be applicable to the ten commandments. We are not taught
that a prudent man will steal upon just occasion, that he
will commit murder in moderation, that he is entitled to
discreet adulteries, that he may season his discourse with
false witness provided it makes for lively gossip, that he
may dishonor his father and his mother so long as it is an
inevitable expression of a generational gap. The commandments are categorical in character, and the only
warrant for an adjustment is when they come into conflict with one another, and we are obliged to appeal to
a higher law.

The simple rule of promptness is intended to be an
absolute. Primarily it is a rule of courtesy. When two
persons have an appointment with one another, it may
also be a matter of courtesy to make allowances for the
one who is late on the assumption that circumstances be-

yond control have prevented his timely appearance. But as the number of persons involved increases, the rule is more strict in application. At a meeting of a committee no one person has a right to keep ten other persons waiting because of a careless tardiness. In this connection it is interesting to note how the rules for promptness in attendance at the theater in the United States have advanced in the rigor of their enforcement over the years. For well over a decade at the Oregon Shakespeare Festival, where the plays are produced outdoors with no intermission whatsoever, it has been a rule that anyone who arrives late will be seated only at the rear, if seats are available, or will not be seated at all. Similar rules are enforced by the American Conservatory Theater in San Francisco. The majority of theatergoers are in favor of this sort of rigor.

In the Epistle to Titus some strict rules are laid down for the elders of the church:

> Observe the tests I prescribed: is he a man of unimpeachable character, faithful to his one wife, the father of children who are believers, who are under no imputation of loose living, and are not out of control? For as God's steward a bishop must be a man of unimpeachable character. He must not be overbearing or short-tempered; he must be no drinker, no brawler, no money-grubber, but hospitable, right-minded, temperate, just, devout, and self-controlled. He must adhere to the true doctrine, so that he may be well able both to move his hearers with wholesome teaching and to confute objectors.[4]

Doubtless there is no such thing as a man of "unimpeachable character," and our judgments are always to be tempered with humility and with charity. It is still good to have the rule which defines the direction of our aspirations.

During a year when I was Dean of the Faculty at Occidental College I was called on by President Arthur Coons to recommend an appointment for track coach. The young man whom I selected turned out to be one of those athletic coaches of whom it could be said in all truth that he was a builder of character. Quite early I noticed the absolute rigor with which he enforced the rules of training; noticed also that every four years he sent some of his men to compete at the Olympic games. Later he became track coach at Stanford University. In 1968 Payton Jordan was made head of the American team at the Olympics in Mexico City. While he always had a great deal to offer his men that was not in the book, I know he would subscribe at the least and absolutely to the teaching in II Timothy, "No athlete can win a prize unless he has kept the rules."[5]

3. *Rules rest on reality.*   This is true of good rules; and, in a world where we are crowded more closely together every day, even rules are subjected to the test of a survival of the fittest. Everyone has made use of a ruler, either to get a straight line, or else to achieve an accurate demarcation of distance. However, if we do much with weights and with measurements, we soon run into the conflict between the English system and the French metric system. The English system appears to have developed casually by rule of thumb (or by rule of foot) and much of the time favors a duodecimal arrangement. The French system is more logical and favors decimal structures. Which is the better? It would cost a lot of money to change a society from one system to the other, and it may be that, with modern computer devices, the problem of effecting translations between the systems is easy to encompass. But few engineers would deny that the metric

system is the better, simply because of its relationship to the realities of arithmetic.

This is a good point in the discussion in which to warn ourselves against the fallacy of origins. This fallacy, which is known colloquially as the "nothing-but fallacy," declares that the value of anything is restricted to the value of where or what it came from. On this theory the ten commandments are good only for a savage tribe of nomads wandering in the wilderness. The teachings of the Sermon on the Mount are good only for a preindustrial economy of scarcity in which people have given up hope for the present and live only in the expectation of a sudden and miraculous end of the world in the near future. Besides, can any good thing come out of Nazareth? By a similar logic many persons have argued that no good thing could come out of Stratford-upon-Avon, and that William Shakespeare could not be the author of his plays and poems. But in history the universal always emerges from a particular locality, whether it be the formula for the law of gravitation, or the personification of love, or a play of human passions, or the drama of The Passion. The final test has nothing to do with the place of origin; it is a test of congruence with reality.

To deal with an ordinary problem: are there any good rules for drinking alcoholic beverages? Even Aristotle would agree that a person who is inclined toward alcoholism should be a total abstainer. Would he agree that, if an entire culture is inclined that way, then it should, as a matter of public policy, promote total abstinence? As for those who believe they are capable of moderation, there are at least two rules that are absolute prohibitions: (1) Never practice solitary drinking; (2) Never drink for consolation. The statistical probability that the breach of either of these two rules will lead to alcoholism is so very high that these rules are simply not to be trifled with. We may now submit a third rule, which will surely be a cause of contention: (3) Never drink in such habitual ways that it becomes imperative for you to have your drink at stated occasions and at stated times. To the degree that one rejects this third rule he begins to list possible friends and impossible associates strictly according to how congenial they are to his habits of drinking. He will, of course, have excluded all devout Mormons, Methodists, and Moslems.

One rule we are supposed to have outgrown in an affluent society is the rule of deferred satisfaction. This is supposed to have been invented by the Puritans, and, since the Puritans have gone, the rule ought to go too. In sex it meant you controlled your appetites until the right man, or the right woman, came along. In finance it meant that, instead of spending your money today, you saved it for investment or for better purchases at a later time. Now in point of fact this rule was invented by the Epicureans long before there were any Puritans in existence. The pleasure-seeking Epicureans early learned to distinguish between present satisfactions and future satisfactions, and to recommend that the prudent man would study how to curb an immediate impulse in order to enjoy a greater satisfaction in the future. Actually the rule of deferred satisfactions is universal in the ethical systems of the world. With the exception of the Cyrenaics, some of the Neo-Taoists, and the extremists in a "now generation," it is constant teaching—Confucian, Christian, Jewish, Moslem, Sinico-Hindu-Hellenic—that a person must observe this rule if he wants to be his own self and not the puppet of instinct, appetite, and impulse. The rule accords with reality.

4. *Rules are universals.* We have already seen that the so-called Puritan rule of deferred satisfaction is, in fact, a universal rule, and deserving of the rank of a moral principle. May not the same be true of what is called the Puritan-Protestant work ethic? This is the ethic of thrift, industry, frugality, hard work, perseverance, initiative, which is supposed to have provided the moral foundations for capitalism. Recently in a discussion of the merits of Israel against its Arab neighbors, I heard it said that of course most Americans must favor the Israelis because the Israelis have this same Protestant work ethic. But where did they, or we, get this work ethic? In fact it came to Christians by way of their heritage from Judaism, and the early literature of the Protestant work ethic is full of references to that part of the Bible which Christians call the Old Testament.

For that matter, commercial capitalism and finance capitalism were not invented in the West. They existed among the Chinese, the Phoenicians, the Jews, long before there was any Christianity. For such people and their like—the Chinese, the Lebanese, the Israelis—there is only one work ethic and it is a universal ethic wherever people want to get a job done efficiently according to some standard of excellence. One might ask why it is that the Japanese and the Germans make such swift recovery after defeat in war. Is it because they, too, have a Protestant work ethic? But West Germany is more Catholic than Protestant, and Japan is neither Protestant nor Christian. In any case in our world the work ethic is an imperative not just for success but for simple survival.

What is going on among the whites and the blacks in the United States today is a curious commentary on this issue. One of the old complaints against the Negro has

been that he is lazy, shiftless, irresponsible, and won't do
his work well. This of course is the inevitable ethic of
slavery because, when the fruit of a man's labor is appropriated by a master, and when the harder a man works
the more brutally he is exploited, he is going to make a
careful study of the arts of indolence on the job. This
heritage from slavery is the white man's fault, but it is the
black man's problem, since only the black man can eman-
cipate himself from this evil. But in the United States
today, while the black man is gladly subjecting himself to
the disciplines of the work ethic, the pampered offspring
of an affluent white middle class begin to persuade themselves that a work ethic is a vulgar irrelevancy to the good
life. So we move rapidly toward a situation in which the
majority of the lazy, the shiftless, the irresponsible, are
not black but white. Whose, then, is the greater slavery?

Surely it is time that we began to liberate ourselves
from the delusions of a cultural relativism. A man who
has traveled only a little will be much impressed by the
differences among peoples. A man who has traveled much
will begin to reflect again on what belongs to our common
humanity. It was a Sunday morning worship service that
finally made me free to enter the larger context. The city
was Honolulu; the people in the congregation were of
Portuguese extraction; the pastor and his wife were pure
corn-fed Iowans from the great American Middle West;
and that day they were celebrating in a Methodist church
the "Aldersgate experience" that happened to a devout
Anglican in an England of more than two centuries ago.
My intellect told me that all this was quite impossible.
How can you get together Hawaii and the Middle West,
the American, the Englishman, the Portuguese, the eighteenth century and the twentieth century, under the aus-

pices of a faith which actually had its origins in faraway
Palestine almost two thousand years ago? But rarely have
I seen such a warm, and faithful, and affectionate fellowship among people. There are universals in our humanity,
and there are some universal rules by which we can live
together.

6

—the Rules of the Game

5. *Rules increase with population pressure.* Anyone who lives in the midst of that complex of academic communities which is Berkeley, California, is bound to be impressed by the diversely codified rules. In general the larger the community, the more self-consciously it is governed by rules; while the smaller community, with its face-to-face relationships, appears not to need that sort of regulation. Recently the University of California, with a student population of 27,500 in Berkeley, has drawn up a list of twelve kinds of misconduct which may be an occasion for discipline: these are, in brief, dishonesty, forgery, theft, damage, physical abuse of persons, obstruction of university activities, unauthorized entry, disorderly conduct, the use of narcotics, the violation of rules of residence or of rules of time, place, and manner, failure to comply with the directions of officials performing their duties, and "conduct which adversely affects the student's suitability as a member of the academic community." If the several theological seminaries in Berkeley, whose populations scarcely average 150 apiece, do not have all these rules, then this is due to a difference not in virtue but in size.

One of the ancient civilizations which early developed an elaborate system of rules was China. Here was a huge country, with an enormous population, and it was necessary to spell out the precise ways in which people would get along together. The Confucian tradition embodies both a code of ethics and a code of etiquette, although it is not clear that the Chinese, any more than the French, would appreciate the Anglo-American distinction between morals and manners. The Confucian code also illustrates a human disposition to multiply rules beyond necessity. But a moralist who makes rules for rules' sake is no worse than an artist who follows art for art's sake. In either case, when the functional relationship of the rules, or of the art, to the rest of culture has been too long neglected, then the time has arrived for a revolution. Certainly Communism in China did well to sweep away a large body of accumulated rules. Just as certainly, Communism has found it necessary to establish new rules of ritual, of ethics, of etiquette, which are probably enforced with more rigor than was ever applied to the old Confucian code.

What is going on in the minds of some American moralists today is indeed most curious. In the early part of our history, so far as our people lived and thought in terms of the frontier, they were in a comparatively ruleless society. But even in such circumstances, with plenty of space available, and with no real crowding together, men found a condition of anarchy intolerable, and were eager to establish constitutions and laws and rules of order. Today, on the other hand, just as we begin to be crowded together and piled up on top of one another in great metropolitan heaps, there are those who would assure us that the time is ripe for a no-rules ethic in which we

are guided by no more than a few elementary impulses
of faith and hope and love. Yet if David Hume in the
eighteenth century could summarize all rules of traffic,
pedestrian and vehicular, in four propositions, while it
takes volumes to cover the same today, are we seriously
to believe that traffic between human beings as persons in
our time has suddenly become simplified rather than
more complicated?

6. *Rules increase with scientific knowledge.*   In parts of
the American Southwest the swimming pool has become
a common attachment to a house or to a motel. Recently
at such a pool, as I read the short list of rules laid down
for its use, it occurred to me that at the good old swimming hole of my youth we habitually violated every one of
these rules. We used to run around the edge of the pool;
we used to duck one another; we would bring food near
the water if we wished; and the girls did not bother to
wear swim caps. I was reminded also of a season on the
beaches of Oregon when I had a conversation with a
friend who was director of physical education at a local
college. I, a philosophy professor, was boasting to my
friend of how I got up in the morning, ran two miles to
the beach, plunged into the cold waters all by myself,
swam around a bit, and then ran back again. My friend
said nothing at the time, but I can still remember the
expression of astonishment and of horror that suddenly
swept over his face and then swiftly vanished. I had of
course broken at least three elementary rules of health
and of security in swimming, and had done so in proud
ignorance. Certainly the formula was applicable to me
that was placed at the bottom of the list of regulations for

that swimming pool in the Southwest: "Only fools ignore the rules."

In most states of the Union, as we go to renew our drivers' licenses every few years, it is with something of a shock that we discover how much fatter is the book of rules than it was the last time. What this means simply is that with more precise knowledge we get more rules and more precise rules. Any sensitive driver is also aware of the unwritten rules that gradually develop. In north Berkeley there are many narrow, winding streets on the sides of the hills; and, if cars are parked on both sides of the street, there is only a single lane in the center where the traffic can move. Already an unwritten rule has arisen that, if two drivers going in opposite ways suddenly confront each other, then the first one to give a directional signal with his hand to the other is to be obeyed absolutely. Under such circumstances there is no time for the exchange of such courtesies as might say, "Not I! but do you please proceed first." Without the unwritten rule traffic would be endlessly stalled.

All of this must raise questions about our liberalistic illusions concerning sexual morality. On the one hand we are being told that we are ready for the "new freedom." On the other hand, we are just beginning to accumulate an enormous body of exact information about our prevailing modes of sexual behavior, and about the effect of this behavior on the mind and the emotions of the person and also on the general welfare of society. What confuses the issue is the argument that increased facilities for freedom—the automobile, the cheap motel, a higher degree of mobility—and an improved technology of birth control—the diaphragm, the intra-uterine device, the pill, the inoculation—must somehow alter our standards of sexual conduct. But while advances in technology may complicate problems and proliferate possibilities, they do not in any way affect the basic moral values concerned. Whether in the traffic of sex and of love or in the traffic of automobiles and of airplanes, an increase of knowledge does lay down a larger number of more precise imperatives concerning the way in which we must act if we hope to achieve results that are humanly significant. So it may well be that the truly new sexual morality will give us more rules than did the Puritan ethic.

7. *Rules are prescriptions of justice.*   Not all rules have to do with courts of justice, but there could be no justice without a system of rules. And the first thing to face here is the necessary and desirable *im*personality of the law. It is an old saying, that the law is no respecter of persons. This means that each individual is to be treated like any other individual, regardless of differences of rank, or of riches, or of color, or of creed, or personal charm. Herein lies the essence of fair play, that everyone should be subject to the same rule. This means that, to some extent, in a court of law we move away from interpersonal "I-Thou" relationships to a relationship between one "It" and another "It." So far as relations in such a court do become personal in character, then we fall back on the devices of influence-peddling, greasing the palm, bribery, and intimidation, in order to get the kind of decision that may suit our private prepossessions.

We may ask, further: If a man seeks justice in a court, what kind of endowments would he hope to find in the judge who is to try his case? What of a judge who should be convinced of the relativity of all rules and of the uniqueness of each situation? Or a judge who should have a heart loaded with love but a mind ignorant of the laws of the land? Or a judge who should be ever so inquisitive about the facts of the case, but should choose to interpret them merely in the light of what he called his faith? Or a judge who should cast off the encumbrance of any constitution, and be content to be guided solely by the promptings of the Holy Ghost? Surely it would be with a terrifying sense of insecurity that any plaintiff would appear before such a judge. But if we seek justice, we desire a judge who knows his rules of procedure, his rules of evidence, and his rules of law.

In the English tradition of common law, the origin of law lies in its acknowledgment of custom. But, since custom cannot be accepted in a promiscuous manner, William Blackstone found it necessary to lay down seven rules for customs: "That they be immemorial . . . That they be continued . . . That they be peaceable . . . That they be reasonable . . . That they be certain . . . That they be compulsive . . . That they be consistent." In speaking of reason and of consistency, Blackstone was introducing criteria of rationality that might better be suited to Roman law. But the reason he had in mind was English common sense, not Latin logic. As for consistency, he urged at first that it would be an absurdity for two customs to contradict each other if both customs were equally immemorial and peaceable (i.e., resting on consent). But then he suggested that, if there should be such a contradiction, one had better deny the existence of one of the customs. So it is that, in the complexity of human affairs, one good law, or custom, or rule, may conflict with another good one; but that does not relieve us of the necessity of forming and of following the rules of the game.

Perhaps now we can understand better what the founding fathers of the American republic meant when they said that they sought to establish a government of laws, not of men. In a purely feudal system, or in a divine-right monarchy, we have a personal government, and the law is simply the edict which issues from the lips of the ruler. Likewise when men follow a charismatic leader, whether he be the chieftain of a revolution or the head of a totalitarian state, they are under a personal government again. But a republic that cares for justice is not a government by any such persons, but a government of rule and of law.

8. *Rules are prescriptions of love.* In its most elementary sense the love of others means simply that we should be considerate of them as persons. All the rules of etiquette, from Confucius to Emily Post or Amy Vanderbilt, have no other end than that. If they go beyond that end, and are elaborated for their own sake, then the rules may be subject to correction. But if they exist as rules, it is because most of our relations to other persons take place in a social context; and it is therefore necessary, as with Blackstone's customs, that there be consent and consistency in how we go about our business. So it is a pleasure, in any part of the world, to meet with someone who knows how to conduct herself or himself as a lady or as a gentleman. And it is a shocking thing to run into a Christian who thinks that, because of the high profession of his religion, he is above being well-mannered. Certainly the higher demands of the law of love will some-

times contradict and transcend the lesser demands, but love does not allow that we should at any time treat another person with contempt.

All the elaborate sets of rules which determine what we shall wear are a part of the elementary etiquette of consideration for others. Just why do we wear clothes? It may seem rudimentary that we wear clothes for comfort and for protection; but, with the most savage and with the most civilized people, it is obvious that much of what they wear is contrary to comfort and unfit for protection. Again, it may be said that we wear clothes in order to express our personalities; yet the range of freedom for this self-expression is strictly delimited by the group. Indeed, there is no group whatsoever, whether it be a drawing room full of high society, or a huddle of hippies, or a gathering of college undergraduates, that does not sharply define what is appropriate dress. In fact, the irreducible imperative about clothes is what we wear them to pay honor to persons or to occasions. It is only an oaf, or an egotist, whose dress is solely for comfort, or for convenience, or for self-expression, and who has no sensitive regard for the persons with whom he finds himself and the circumstances which bring them all together. Therefore, in the parable of the wedding feast, when the king finds a guest who is not attired in a wedding garment, he decrees: "Bind him hand and foot, and take him away, and cast him into outer darkness; there shall be weeping and gnashing of teeth."[1]

But it is not merely love on the elementary level of considerateness for others that has its rules and prescriptions. Even love in all the fullness of Christian aspiration has its specifications. So the apostle writes:

Love is patient; love is kind and envies no one. Love is
never boastful, nor conceited, nor rude; never selfish, not
quick to take offense. Love keeps no score of wrongs; does
not gloat over other men's sins, but delights in the truth.
There is nothing love cannot face; there is no limit to its
faith, its hope, and its endurance.[2]

Three observations are to be made here. First of all, Saint
Paul's description of love is strictly behavioristic. He is
not talking about a mystical entity. He is talking about
what is public, observable, and verifiable. In the second
place, while the rules do not make love, still love is known
by its regard for the rules. And anything that calls itself
love but is impatient, unkind, envious, quick to take offense, contemptuous of the truth, ready to gloat over the
failings of others, and unable to stand up under the emergencies of life, is not really love. In the third place, Paul's
list of prescriptions for love is not excessive; it is probably inadequate and incomplete.

9. *The man of breeding has built-in rules.*   One way to
devise a comedy is to have a character who confronts a
situation that calls for quick action, and who then pulls
a book of rules from his pocket, and begins desperately
to thumb through it looking for the directions that will
help him out of his difficulty. The emergency might be
one of driving a car, or one of making love to a woman.
What is ludicrous in the situation is that there is no time
to look up the rules. What is ludicrous also is that our
character is behaving like a pedant, "by the book," when
he ought to be acting swiftly like a man of good judgment. The same comedy could be elaborated if, instead
of a book of rules, the character should be consulting a
memorized and organized set of rules in his head, and

should proceed to a careful analysis and sorting out of
the rules until he has found the right one—much too late
for it to be useful. The point is that the rules ought not
now to be in the book, or even in one's head. They ought
to be in the synapses, in the conditioned reflexes, in the
habitual modes of behavior.

When the Confucian code of ethics and of etiquette
was first introduced in Japan, some of the Japanese
scholars were greatly scandalized. They argued that the
Chinese must be a very immoral people if they had to
be governed by such an intricately elaborate set of rules.
On the other hand, it was maintained that the Japanese,
with their natural endowment of goodness, spontaneously
understood correct behavior without benefit of instruction from a book. What all this went to prove, however,
was simply a difference in the size of the two countries.
In a small, compact territory like Japan one could depend
upon the pervasive and uniform power of custom to take
care of the task of good breeding. But in an enormous
area like China, with diversities in culture between north
and south and east and west, it was necessary to articulate
the rules in a literary tradition that could be consciously
learned as well as unconsciously practiced.

Once in a rock cavern in rose-red Petra in Jordan, I
found myself in conversation with a young Englishman,
who was disposed to be critical of the morality of the
establishment in his country. I had the pleasure of giving
him a defense and eulogy of the English character. I
mentioned the good sportsmanship of the English, their
sense of fair play; their cheerfulness in adversity; their
patience in the long hard pull; their *sang froid* and their
ability to play it cool. At each of these items my young
friend made a gesture as though to dismiss it from the

conversation, as something to be taken for granted but not worth any particular discussion. But it was only because he was an Englishman that he could take it for granted. It was a part of his breeding. It is not part of the breeding of the Latin people. As for Americans—we have learned what good sportsmanship we have from the English. But in adversity we gripe rather than act cheerful, we are proud of our impatience, and we are more prompt to hysteria than to play it cool. Who has the better rules, and which is the better breeding?

In the Old Testament book of the prophet Jeremiah and also in the New Testament book of the Epistle to the Hebrews, there is a parallel teaching. God speaks of a new covenant that will be placed in the inward parts of his people and written in their hearts. They will not then need to be taught the law of the Lord, because they will already know it.[3] They will have been born persons of good breeding.

10. *Rules liberate.* The last time that I took a written test to renew my driver's license in the State of California, I found myself faced with some 225 rules in the booklet issued by the bureau of motor vehicles. In part what irked me was that some of these rules had long since left my head and were safely embedded in my conditioned reflexes, but now I had to get them back into my head. I was irked also by the fact that there were quite a few new rules, and that some of the familiar rules had been modified slightly so that they had to be learned again in their new form. However, as I studied for the test I made myself cheerful by keeping two questions firmly in mind: "Will, or will not, the learning of these rules make a better driver of me? If I conform to these

rules, shall I, or shall I not, be able better to reach whatever destination I please?" It seemed obvious that the answer to both of these questions was in the affirmative.

Certainly our discussion of the role of rules today has got us into a curiously unrealistic position. We are surrounded by apostles of a new morality who want to make us free by liberating us from the rules. But it is the rules that make us free. More than this, far from restricting our liberties, the rules are so inadequate to most life situations that they still leave gaping before us a horrible void of freedom in which we are compelled to exercise an unwonted degree of creativity. Who is there who in driving a car, or in making love, or in conducting a business enterprise, or in being engaged in a fight, or in playing a game of ball, or in carrying out his duties as a citizen or as a ruler, has not confronted such startling emergencies that he has wished only that there were a book of rules to tell him what to do? But now there are no rules; there is only the clean emptiness of an utter liberty.

Every creative enterprise is a blend of discipline and of freedom. It is the discipline with which we begin. If it be said that the discipline will choke off the freedom, then such a sort of freedom was scarcely worth preserving in the first place. Indeed, it is possible, in our world of romantic delusions, that too many of us want to be creators, and not enough of us are content to be good craftsmen. Any scholar, any mechanic, any musician, knows the experience of the long, early grind in which he subjects himself to the studies, the routines, the exercises which can be so intolerably tedious, but which are the necessary preliminaries to the skill he would acquire. Then suddenly comes the day, not always recognized at the moment of its arrival, when one is no longer the sub-

ject of the rules but the master of them, and one is at
last free to understand, to use, to enjoy according to the
impulses of one's own creativity.

Love also has its rules and disciplines. Whether I
would be an athlete on the playing field or an athlete
for Christ, I should know that the *regula* comes before the
liberty. Saint Paul understood this much. If he had been
as good a Jew, or a Catholic, as he was a Protestant, he
might have understood it better.[4] As for myself, I like to
remember how, once a month in our home in Hangchow,
an old bowed Chinese scholar came to call, to drink a
cup of tea and to receive the gift of a silver dollar for
his present support. My father had already gone way
beyond his tutor in a mastery of the reading and writing
of the Mandarin character. But my father did not forget
to be grateful to his first teacher.

7

Love as the Law of Life

It is in the 119th Psalm that we get one of the most eloquent statements of the classical Jewish delight in the law of the Lord. Here it is made clear that every one of God's precepts and commandments is precious in itself. The author grows lyrical in his adulation of God's word as it is revealed in his law: "Thy word is a lamp to my feet and a light to my path," and, again, "Thy statutes have been my songs in the house of my pilgrimage." This law is not imposed as an alien force on the self, but is rather an expression of the innermost nature of the self. So the writer exclaims, "Oh, how I love thy law!"[1]

In Matthew, Jesus says that he has come not to destroy the law but to fulfill it. So he distinguishes between ethical imperatives and ritual requirements. He seeks to get at the inner motives behind the commandments: the lust that underlies adultery, the hatred that leads to murder. He discards the accretions of tradition in order to get back to the original precepts. And he attempts to simplify the moral code in order to get at the essential, which is the law of love. In no sense does he repudiate the divine imperative; nor is there any evidence whatsoever that he was promoting a no-rules ethic.

Saint Paul had the same passion for getting at the root of the matter—for simplifying the details, and for seeking out the sources of power. Yet he made it plain that the ten commandments are taken for granted under the law of love,[2] and he was vehement in his denunciation of those who "break all rules of conduct."[3] Indeed, while his list of the "fruits of the Spirit" never exceeded a maximum of nine,[4] one can find in the epistles some forty different acts of evil which come under his vehement execrations. If Protestant followers of Paul sometimes tumble into antinomianism, they do not do so by his example.

Absolutism Versus Relativism

The argument today usually takes the impossible form of a debate between absolutism and relativism. The absolutist says there is an objective and universal moral law which holds for all persons at all times and in all places. This is supported by the Greek belief in a cosmos instead of a chaos, by the medieval view of the laws of God, and by the Newtonian view of the laws of nature. It gathers further support from the witness of non-Christian religions, which affirm that a Law of Heaven or a Law of the Deed is operative in the lives of all men. It is hard to believe that all this evidence, converging from so many different quarters, does not testify to some underlying reality.

Unfortunately the absolutism, which is so sublime in theory, contradicts itself in practice. One might speak here of the "axiom of the nth degree": any value when carried to its extreme limit will destroy itself. If, like Napoleon or Hitler, you make an absolute of power, you end up in weakness. If, like America in the 1920's, you make an absolute of prosperity, you end up in poverty. If, like the Cyrenaics and the hedonists, you pursue pleasures unending, you end up with pain. If you turn truth into an absolute, it hardens into dogma and becomes a lie. If you cherish liberty unlimited, as Plato observed, you get anarchy and then a new slavery. There is no value, good or evil, that can escape such an outcome if it is absolutized.

On the other hand, the relativist can always make a plausible argument for his position. He denies that there are any universal and objective values, and declares that all is relative to time and to place. In a commercial economy like ours it may be important to define the meaning of honesty; but neither Jesus nor Aristotle says anything about it, because both lived in a feudal, agricultural economy. In an economy of scarcity gluttony may be one of the seven deadly sins that can put a man in hell, but it would hardly rate such honors in an economy of abundance. And, incidentally, just what is the meaning of honor today? I find very few persons who can give it a coherent content. Yet in a feudal military society honor has very exact meanings both for a man and for a woman, and no person—unless he were as heroically disreputable as a Falstaff—would want to be caught in contempt of this honor.

Unfortunately relativism is subject to the same "axiom of the nth degree" which governs absolutism. In practice it annihilates itself. For if there are no universal and objective standards, if everything is just a question of what I like and of what you like, what really happens? In an affluent society, where there is plenty to go around for everybody, we may practice the principle of "live and let live." This is the privilege and the illusion of the soft relativists. But in the world at large, where there is crowding, poverty, and famine, and where what you like and what I like must come into conflict with one another, the tough relativists are those who will hold sway. For they understand that relativism must really return to the most ancient and evil of all absolutisms—the rule that might makes right.

THE SITUATIONIST ETHICS

A school of thought which would play the mediator in this dispute is called situationism. It emphasizes the relativities of the various situations in which we find ourselves, but holds onto the absolute imperative of love. There is of course nothing new in the notion that one situation differs from another. Aristotle was most insistent on this point. He is constantly reminding us that we must consider the time and place and manner and means and motive and agent in every act. At the same time he believed in an objective moral order, and was very much concerned to elaborate the principles and the rules by which that order might be made explicit in each situation. In these matters there is nothing in the teaching of the *Nicomachean Ethics* that will not fit in with the classical tradition in Christian ethics.

While the situationist stress on love as an absolute is really as old as the rather naïve Protestant liberalism of the 1920's, at this particular moment it makes the impact of some newly liberating evangel. Why is this so? The important thing in its popular appeal is the deletion of rules and principles and an attitude toward the ten commandments which combines cursory respect with a casual disregard. So we get an apologetic for anarchy, a sanction for moral chaos, in which we have let loose upon us a band of evangelists of love who are persuaded that, so long as their hearts are loaded with the sublime emotion, then anything they do must be right regardless of how much it may contravene the ordinary rules of behavior. Unfortunately the apostles of this cult do not always share in the Christian heritage of their teacher, nor in the faith and discipline of his own acknowledged Master.

There is, indeed, a technical error in situationism which must be held responsible for these excesses. This doctrine fails to make enough of the several universal situations to which we belong always and everywhere. There is our situation as children of the living God, made in his image. It can make some difference in our treatment of others whether or not we acknowledge this situation. There is our situation as children of nature; and, while we might dispute the meaning of that between an Aristotle and a Rousseau, between a Darwin*ist* and a Thomas Huxley, none of us can deny this situation. There is our situation as the heirs of history and of tradition. This history can no longer be the parochial history of one people or of one place, but it is a universal history in the traditions of which we all participate. There is finally our situation as human beings. No one, whether he comes from the north or the south, from the east or the west, can deny his share in a common humanity. To pretend to treat of particular situations without regard to these universal situations is to trivialize and to confuse our specific moral judgments.

One phenomenon that goes with the fashionable cult of ethical relativism is the capricious absolutist. This is a person who makes an absolute claim for some value in reaction or in reform, but is unable to relate it to a universal imperative in morals. A subspecies of this class of ethical caprice is the *un*conscientious objector. A conscientious objector is one who acts from a fixed body of principle, is willing to take the full consequences of his action, and shows a persistence in behavior that comes from real commitment. But the *un*conscientious objector meets none of these conditions; he simply objects because he objects.

God's Law and Nature's Law

However, if there is a universal and objective moral law, as we maintain here, what is the nature of that law, and how is it related to the laws of nature?

First of all, let it be remarked that the status of this law and its revelation are the same for science as for religion. The law of gravitation existed from the time of the first shaping of the heavenly bodies. It was "revealed" by an Isaac Newton, who crystallized it into a compact mathematical formula. The law of creative growth, or the law of love, was always the operative law for human nature. It was "revealed" and made incandescent in the incarnation of the Christ. Before the revelation of the law —of nature, or of human nature—men had only a tentative and fumbling grasp on its reality. After the revelation people suddenly had the capacity to act with an enhanced vision and with an accelerated power. But whether in nature or in human nature our initial ignorance of the law has nothing to do with its self-enforcing qualities. The law has always been there whether we acknowledged it or not.

Now it may be insisted that modern science gives us a

more sophisticated view of natural law than is found in Newtonian mechanics. True enough, a contemporary view would insist that natural laws are descriptive rather than prescriptive; that they are statistical in character and therefore always have exceptions; that they are relative to a frame of reference; that, at rates which vary greatly from one frame to another, they are slowly evolving; that their final function for us is instrumental and liberating.

Nevertheless, for all this sophistication in theory, most of us live most of the time in the world of Newtonian mechanics. The refinements that belong to the areas of macro-physics and of micro-physics doubtless find parallels in some of the refinements that we get today in the realms of what should be called macro-ethical or micro-ethical speculation. Those of us who are neither pygmies nor giants would do well, in company with the great skeptic David Hume, to return ourselves to the world of common sense when it comes to affairs of daily life. To think that my case is so grand or so special that I can transcend the law of love and its rules and commandments is as foolish as to think that I can step safely out of a fifth-story window and walk into the air because the law of gravitation has been abrogated in a higher synthesis.

To be sure, when we deal with morals, the language of philosophy is not always the language of religion. For religion, which keeps quite close to daily life, it is well to speak of the law of love. For philosophy it is helpful to speak of the law of creative growth. This law is marked by various polarities. A basic one is that between crisis and continuity, between revolution and steady evolution. Other polarities in value are between liberty and discipline, pleasure and pain, security and adventure, competition and cooperation. To go all out for just one end of any one of these polarities is a certain way to invite disaster. The problem is how to keep a tension between them that is creative rather than destructive. Also we must take warning against short-term cancerous growths, against any neurotic delight in change for its own sake, and learn to identify ourselves with growth on the whole and in the long run.

Creative growth differs from classical absolutes in ethics in two important ways. It has a built-in regard for the fact of change and a criterion for coping with change. It is pluralistic in its impact rather than monistic. Several basic values enter into creative growth. Love, justice, liberty, truth, beauty, all belong here. It is also the case that their direct opposites—hatred, injustice, slavery, lies, ugliness—are inherently evil. But as pluralists we must remember that no one of these values automatically embraces all the rest. And here we differ radically from Christian neoliberalism, or situationism, in ethics. God's love may be perfect; man's love never is. Certainly the first choice for man is the choice between love and hate. But it is then necessary always to check his actions of love against objective standards and rules that may safeguard him from perpetrating, in the name of love, some illicit liberty or some ugly injustice.

COMPROMISE ON PRINCIPLE

Creative growth, because of its inherently pluralistic character, always calls for the balance of competing goods. In fact all the important decisions in ethics involve this sort of judgment. If it is just a question of making a stark choice between good and evil, love and hate, lies and truth, there is not much of a problem. The difficulty arises when we have to weigh the competing claims of liberty and equality, of love and justice, of security and adventure; or, worse yet, when we have to work out a practical solution that will protect a maximum number of values even while it inevitably excludes other values that are also precious. This everyday complication of the ethical problem is something that Immanuel Kant, with his naïve monism, never understood.

Truth is a sacred value; but, when the Scriptures tell us to speak the truth in love,[5] they are making things difficult. One can, for instance, speak the truth in malice. William Blake wrote:

> A truth that's spoke with bad intent
> Is worse than all the lies you can invent.

Do we speak the truth in humility, or in courage, or in self-righteousness? For myself I have worked out a sliding scale between truth and love, with four rules to govern four different situations. For the word that is written in a book, and therefore somewhat impersonal, speak the truth as plainly as possible and let love follow after. For the word spoken in a classroom, where the hearers are right before you, let there be more of love. For the word spoken from the pulpit, which goes to a congregation with a common fellowship in the most intimate and the most noble endeavors, let love and truth be in equal proportions. For the word uttered in a committee meeting, let there be lots of love, and be content if a little bit of truth triumphs occasionally just from time to time.

While truth is precious, so is peace. Unfortunately the speaking of the truth will sometimes function as a disturber of the peace. Roger Williams was conscious of this when, in his famous essay against persecution for cause of conscience, he put Truth and Peace in dialogue in opposition to one another. The love of peace can also stand in opposition to the love of liberty and of justice. This is what defines one of the perennial debates within the Christian family. At the time war has already been declared, which is the more loving act, or the act most in accord with creative growth, or the act which preserves a maximum of values on the whole and in the long run: to stand fast for peace at the expense of some liberty and some justice, or to fight for liberty and justice and to let peace go for a while?

Appeasement is something quite other than this sort of calculated compromise. Appeasement comes from the context of relativism rather than from the context of pluralism within the frame of reference of creative growth. Appeasement is not action from principle, but action from cowardice before a superior force. Appeasement sacrifices anything for an immediate end, and is oblivious to all long-range consequences. In the case of appeasement there is no good faith between the parties concerned, since what we have here is a transaction between naked power on the one hand and some sort of fatuous idealism on the other hand. In the outcome the appeaser is always weakened—morally because he has betrayed his trust, intellectually because he has deceived himself. The appeaser, like Parolles in *All's Well That Ends Well*, wants only to be allowed to live a few more moments, even at the cost of truth, of honor, of liberty, of all self-respect.

Therefore, within the context of creative growth, compromise is not a bad name but a necessary act. There is the perennial compromise between human frailty and the ideals which we would serve. There is compromise within a common frame of reference, where we agree on fundamentals but differ on some lesser matters. There is also compromise in the situation where we have sharp disagreements with one another, but can still find some common ground for communication. And every day in every way there is the compromise between competing goods, none of which can be claimed in its totality both because of the finitude of man and because of the alterations of time. But this is compromise on principle, by means of principle, with the aid of rules, commandments, and statutes—i.e., compromise under law.

OF LIBERTY AND OF LAW

If there is a universal and objective moral order—call it creative growth, or call it the law of love—what happens to human freedom? Here it is necessary to combine the insight of classical Judaism with the insight of Pauline Christianity. We may say that this law is self-legislated, because it expresses my nature as a child of God. It is for this reason that I can delight in the law of the Lord. On the other hand, so far as one is a sinner who rejects the law of love, then the law comes to him as a commandment from without, because now there is a breach between the Creator and the creature that was made in his image.

As for the exercise of man's freedom of will, or freedom of choice and responsible decision, it always takes place on two levels. There is our freedom to choose to love or to hate, to grow or to rot, to create or to destroy. Then, if we have chosen the way of love, of growth, of creativity, there follows an infinite series of decisions in which we have to discover just how love is to be fulfilled with such persons in such situations in such times and in such places.

On this second level, the amount of liberty available to us
may even be terrifying in its proportions. In a profounder
sense, apart from these two considerations, the law of
love is a law that has liberty written at the very heart of
it, for, as we shall see, it is only love that truly liberates.

So far as we live out this law as children of God and live
under this law as sinners, there is always the need of
God's grace and for man's graciousness. God's grace
shows itself as mercy toward us for our shortcomings and
as a power added to us by which we can do more than
we would have expected to do. Man's graciousness is an
exercise in humility and in charity—a forgiveness of the
frailty in others and a remembrance of the sinfulness in
ourselves.

In our understanding of this law we need to exercise
imagination as much as intellect in order to grasp its
larger meanings. There are three psalms which I now
choose to call the Birmingham Psalms. They are the
psalms—27, 37, 91—which the black pastor called on his
people to go home and read when a bomb burst in his
church and killed some little children. Psalm 37:25 reads:
"I have been young, and now am old; yet have I not seen
the righteous forsaken, nor his seed begging bread."[6] In
the immediate situation lines like that seem to be cruel
and outrageous nonsense. But perhaps the black pastor,
and perhaps even the Jewish psalmist before him, understood these words in a larger and a universal situation.

We may need to free our minds again from literalism
and to entertain an ampler vision if we are to recover the
truth in the majestic exhortations of Deuteronomy. Doubtless when we choose between life and death, between love
and hate, the blessing and the curse that fall upon our
body, our basket, our fields, and our flocks will not come

so swiftly nor with such material force as the text indicates. But we are still called upon to confront the same
alternatives which are uttered by the voice which cries
out: "I call heaven and earth to record this day against
you, that I have set before you life and death, blessing
and cursing: therefore choose life, that both thou and thy
seed may live: That thou mayest love the LORD thy God,
and that thou mayest obey his voice, and that thou mayest
cleave unto him: for he is thy life . . ."[7]

For he is thy life. And love is the law of thy life as of
his.

8

Love's Means and Ends

Before we go on with the distinctively Biblical witness about the meaning of love, there are two technical problems in ethics that claim our attention. One has to do with the relation of motives to consequences; the other, with the relation of means to ends. These two problems are intertwined with each other. While there is no formal discussion of them in the Scriptures, there are nevertheless some important emphases.

THE MEANING OF MOTIVES

There are two quite different uses of the appeal to motives. One appeal is a device of irresponsibility. It seems that we are always being "misunderstood." Why is it that people misinterpret our motives so outrageously? So it is that the older generation fails to understand the younger generation, and the younger generation fails to understand the older. The husband misunderstands his wife, and the wife misunderstands the husband. Teachers and pupils misunderstand one another, as do pastors and their congregations, and politicians and their constituencies. Nowadays all this is blamed on a failure to communicate.

To all this business some very plain words need to be spoken. First of all, it is a mark of infantilism to seek perfect understanding. This is something we thought we had as children when we were sure that mother understood everything. On the other hand, it is possible that, when we complain of not being understood, we are in fact being understood only too well. Indeed, others may understand us better than we do ourselves. They see too clearly in us the self-centered faults that we are unwilling to acknowledge. Finally, the basic responsibility is mine —to make myself understood, whether I am teacher, writer, politician, pastor, or lover. The fact that people do not then immediately agree with me does not mean that I have failed to communicate. I may have communicated all too well. Jesus was a most effective communicator. Some of those who understood him gave him love; others who understood him wanted to crucify him.

There is another kind of appeal to motives, the kind used by our Lord, which is an effort to get at the springs of conduct. This accounts for the radical sayings in the Sermon on the Mount concerning murder and adultery.[1] The commandment not to do murder still stands, but Jesus means to give us a sharp warning against the wrath and the hatred in the heart which may lead to murder. The commandment against adultery still stands, but in a sharp and hyperbolical statement Jesus warns against the lust in the heart which will lead to adultery. So it is that we are called upon to be pure in heart. If what comes out of the heart is not clean, then the consequences will not be clean.

Besides the particular motives that govern our conduct, there is a fundamental motive. This is expressed in the two great commandments: to love God with all our heart and soul and mind, and to love our neighbor as ourself.[2] If our heart is truly filled with this sort of love, and if this love becomes the mainspring of all our conduct, then we are pure in heart. Whether or not any man, even with the help of God's grace, can achieve such a perfect purity of heart in this life is an important question. At any rate, the teaching of Jesus indicates the direction our endeavors should take.

This discussion of the springs of action may help us to understand another teaching of the church that is related to conduct. When the priority of faith over works is stressed, this is not to belittle the works, but to get at the springs of action. The faith indicated here is not assent to creedal propositions. It is an act of self-surrender to the love of God revealed in Jesus Christ. It is this self-surrender which provides the motive power and the definition to all that we do. Without such motive power we may work hard at the works of love, and either deceive ourselves into thinking that we have done a lot when we have not, or, more likely, discover that our works of love don't really come off very well because they do not spring from the true sources of the power to love.

THE TEST OF FRUITS

While the motives of man are what we need in order to get him moving, they do not provide a clue for judgments of the good and the bad. Motives taken in themselves are too easily imputed. Whatever I do of course springs from the innate virtue, innocence, and nobility of my disposition; and I shall feel hurt and misunderstood if others fail to see this as I do. On the other hand, when I am resolved to have someone as an enemy, then I can impute evil motives to him in an identical piece of business whether he gets it done or leaves it undone. Motives *per se* are not public, observable, and verifiable. They are not open to inspection.

This is why the teaching of Jesus is categorical for the test of fruits. "Even so every good tree bringeth forth good fruit; but a corrupt tree bringeth forth evil fruit. . . . Every tree that bringeth not forth good fruit is hewn down, and cast into the fire. Wherefore by their fruits ye shall know them."[3] It is not just in the Sermon on the Mount that this is made emphatic. It appears also in the teaching of the Last Judgment. In the final separation of the sheep from the goats, the damned are those who believe they meant well but in fact did poorly, while the saved are those who did well even though they did not know that they meant so well.[4]

With Saint Paul, who wants to get away from a narrow legalism, there is still the problem of specifying just what fruits come from the Holy Spirit and which ones come from an unholy spirit. At times his imagination seems to run riot in an enumeration of the fruits that are evil, but he wants a simpler list of the fruits that are good. In one epistle, after naming fifteen kinds of bad behavior, he gives us nine good ones: "love, joy, peace, patience, kindness, goodness, fidelity, gentleness, and self-control."[5] However, in a systematic treatment of spiritual gifts in the First Epistle to the Corinthians he gets down to "three things that last for ever: faith, hope, and love,"

and then concludes that "the greatest of them all is
love."[6] This love, moreover, is not just an attitude nor
a feeling, but in four verses is defined objectively with
behavioristic precision.[7]

In the simple language of the Gospels, it is important
to know the difference between hearing and saying and
doing. In spite of some distortions that come to us from
a part of the Protestant tradition, it is plain that for Jesus
the doing is definitive. At this point he speaks as an heir
of classical Judaism. "Not every one that *saith* unto me,
Lord, Lord, shall enter into the kingdom of heaven; but
he that *doeth* the will of my Father which is in heaven."
And his great sermon comes to a climax in the tale of the
foolish man who built his house on the sand—"And every
one that *heareth* these sayings of mine, and *doeth them
not* . . ."—and the wise man who built his house on a
rock—"whosoever *heareth* these sayings of mine, *and
doeth* them . . ."[8]

Each parable, or saying, of Jesus usually has just one
point, and not half a dozen. So there is nothing in the
emphasis on fruits and consequences to contradict the
story about Mary and Martha.[9] When Jesus came to call
on them, Martha was too busy with household tasks to
have time for him; but Mary, who understood the one
thing needful, sat at his feet to hear his word. Martha
was too busy with worldly cares at a time when she should
have been able to put them aside for the opportunity to
receive God's teaching and to refresh the springs of conduct in her own life. But for Mary or Martha, for Peter or
John, the final test of true discipleship is that they will
then rise up, and gird their loins, and run the race, and at
last drink of his cup and bear his cross.[10]

MEANS AND ENDS

When we talk about motives and consequences, we also talk perforce about means and ends, because ends and consequences and outcomes are one and the same thing. Indeed, developing the right sort of motivation may be one of the problems of the means to an end. However, there are several issues here that need clarification.

A prevailing tradition in ethics holds it to be unacceptable that the end justifies the means. Usually this is thought of as a sort of Machiavellian teaching—that, if you want to gain power, or impose peace, or obtain wealth, then any sort of means is justified provided you get what you wanted in the first place. Here we need to be reminded that there can be the lunatics of love who, being confident of their own perfect purity of heart, and being firmly persuaded that their end-in-view is the loving one of establishing at once a Kingdom of God on earth, where justice and righteousness and brotherhood will flourish, may, like the Puritans satirized in *Hudibras,* think "fire and sword and desolation A godly, thorough reformation." It seems that some of these fanatics of love are with us again, though in a more secular guise.

But if we deny that the end justifies the means, we must also reject the contemporary doctrine that the means is the end. One form that this takes in the world of communications is the notion that the medium is the message. Here it is argued that the means by which we express ourselves really determine the ends of our utterances. Since television is marked by immediacy of communication, we are assured that it must determine in itself what is to be communicated, while the devices of speech and of writing fall increasingly into desuetude. Curiously enough, the propagator of this doctrine makes his money chiefly by lecturing and by writing books. In any case this dogma is typical of a mechanistic age. The true artist always bends the medium to make it express his message.

Another aspect of the doctrine that the means is the end is found in the modern intoxication with power. Everybody thinks that if he can just seize power somehow or other—whether it be black power, or white power, or student power, or professors' power, or political power —then he can get whatever he wants. Let us grant that power, in some form, is the means par excellence. But when it is no longer subordinated to wisdom and justice and love, when we make a drunken idolatry of it so that it becomes in itself the Chief End of Man, then we fall into stark Satanism.

John Dewey is the only philosopher I know who has said the essential about means and ends. His first observation is that means and ends are organic to one another. This may help us to understand in what sense love is both a means and an end. If we have a proper regard for our ends, then we shall be careful to select the means that really serve them rather than destroy them. For the means we choose will certainly have an effect on the end we envisage. So one may begin by doing the right thing, but also by doing it in the wrong way. If so, the time comes when the right thing becomes the wrong thing, because the end has been corrupted by the means. Perhaps the American involvement in Vietnam would illustrate this point.

Dewey's other observation is that every action in which we engage always has several outcomes. In point of fact there is no such thing as the end; there are always plural ends. And there is an important sense in which these ends feed into one another, so that endings go on without end. Dewey therefore indicates an important distinction between two sets of consequences. One is the intended consequence, or the end-in-view; the other has to do with the unintended or collateral consequences. What we always have in mind, of course, is the end-in-view; and we think we are smart if we have chosen a means that will effect that end. Nevertheless, the collateral consequences are always there too.

The means therefore are justified, or not justified, by all their ends, outcomes, consequences. If the end-in-view was good, but if the collateral consequences are overwhelmingly harmful, then the means have not been justified.

MORAL RESPONSIBILITY

This understanding of means and ends helps us to arrive at a definition of moral responsibility that may be helpful. First of all, we must insist on the reality of the freedom of the will, without which there can be no moral responsibility. This is our freedom to choose between alternatives, to make a responsible decision. It is a freedom that is affirmed by both the Hebraic and the Hellenic traditions that shape our culture. The story of man in the Garden of Eden, the great exhortation in Deuteronomy, the sayings and parables of Jesus, take for granted this power of choice. Aristotle was one of the first to wrestle with the problem philosophically in his *Nicomachean Ethics*. At that time the issue had not yet received clear definition, but Aristotle understood perfectly well its practical applications.

For theology it has been an historic problem, to recon-
cile man's freedom with God's omnipotence. If man is
truly free, then there must be a limit somewhere to God's
foreknowledge and power. If God is truly all-knowing
and all-powerful, then man's daily course of conduct must
be predetermined, and his final fate predestined. The
only solution to the problem is a dialectical one. Like
Immanuel Kant we recognize that, when we cope with
ultimate questions, we run into antinomies. We find that
we can prove, or disprove, either or both sides of the same
argument. In practice the Calvinists arrived at a pragmatic solution. On the one hand, they insisted on the
absolute sovereignty of God. On the other hand, they
insisted on strict accountability for human conduct.

To be sure, there are stages in the development of
moral responsibility. It is typical of the child that it accepts responsibility for the outcome of none of its actions.
If trouble ensues, the child runs to the arms of the mother,
who provides perfect understanding. There are persons
of more advanced years who still exhibit these childish
characteristics. If they come from one of the underprivileged sectors of our society—the very poor, the very
rich, or the comfortable middle classes—there will be
sympathetic folk on hand to argue that, of course, the
poor chap has no sense of responsibility for his conduct.
If so, then the fault lies with parents, teachers, preachers,
deans, policemen, judges, who have failed to hold him
responsible. Because no child learns responsibility unless
the agencies of society bring it home. For the child, as for
the small puppy, the first lessons in responsibility are be-
wildering and painful; they hurt, and they don't make any
sense. Here suffering must precede understanding.

A second stage in growth is the readiness to accept responsibility for the intended consequence, or the end-in-view. This can be quite an achievement since, as Schopenhauer remarked, we often do not want what we wanted once we get it. It is, however, the mark of the zealot, of the fanatic, to consider only the end-in-view and to hold in contempt all the other consequences of his conduct. A mature person must be willing to accept responsibility for the collateral consequences. Since we cannot be omniscient in our prescience, there will always be collateral consequences of an unpredictable and startling character. Here we are simply obliged to do the best we can with whatever outcomes there may be for good or for evil.

The fully mature person, however, goes beyond this. He accepts responsibility for social consequences that are not of his doing. Whether these take the form of poverty, disease, war, racial prejudice, the decay of cities, he will bear his part in doing what can be done to remedy an evil. Nor is there any injustice here, because, without thinking about it, this person has already "accepted responsibility" for the good things which came to him free of charge in his social heritage. He has been willing to benefit, without complaint, from freedom, affluence, good health, educational opportunities, constitutional democracy, and the best fruits of science and of religion. This larger responsibility derives from the fact of our inescapable life in community—that man is by nature a *zoon politikon,* a political animal; that we all belong in some sense to a people of Israel.

MORAL MATURITY

Finally the question arises as to what bearing all these considerations may have on our understanding of moral maturity. In an absolute sense, moral maturity is a myth which may inspire conduct but which may also distort it.

By definition an adolescent is someone who is not yet mature. If the adolescent knows this, then he may be better off than some folk who parade themselves as mature minds. Indeed, there are adolescents of all ages. We are speaking of an affair that is psychological more than chronological. One mark of the adolescent may be an overconfidence in his powers—"I can take care of myself all right"—but the mature person knows the limits of his capacities and the sometimes irresistible caprice of circumstance. Since an adolescent is in the process of finding himself in part by breaking away from authority, he is automatically ready to resist the establishment, is hypersensitive about his personal liberties, and is eager to bear more than his share in decision-making on every level. He also assumes that maturity is what one claims as a right rather than having to earn it painstakingly. So it has been said, "An adolescent is someone who acts like a child when you refuse to treat him like an adult."

The prevailingly popular view of the mature person, however, may be little more than a projection of adolescent wish fulfillment. To be sure it has a long lineage from Aristotle to Harry Allen Overstreet. This view locates the center of maturity in the mind, and sees the ideal person as one who is poised, rational, and self-controlled. It is an ideal which fascinated Shakespeare in his youth, which provoked his envy when he saw it fulfilled in others but not in himself, and which prompted and partly defined an exploration of character that runs through all his plays. In two of the great tragedies we see that maturity of rational self-control is found in an Horatio but not in a Hamlet; that it exists superbly in an Iago, while an Othello

fails in it tragically. But which of these is the more complete human being? If the essential is to achieve poise and
rational self-control, then Iago is the perfect example. He
manages it by expelling from his breast the impulses of
love and of duty, and by killing in himself all the worthwhile human emotions.

Let us acknowledge, then, that maturity by this definition will only give us a monster, and that most persons
we cherish are only partly mature as they are partly im-
mature. Abraham Lincoln in politics achieved a maturity
way beyond that of any other public figure in American
life; yet there was a persistent melancholia and imma-
turity in his emotional makeup that seriously affected his
early business enterprises as well as his relations with his
wife and children. Socrates was probably the greatest
teacher that ever lived; but he devoted his whole career
to what we now call the "bull session," and never developed the "mature philosophy" of a Plato or an Aristotle.
Henry Ford I was a mechanical genius with a magnificent
vision of the possibilities of the technical liberation of
American society; but in his political judgments he was
worse than infantile, and in his last years his resistance to
change almost ruined the great business he had founded.

The essential in the definition of a person is his loves.
Whether or not the greatest feats of love belong to the
mature mind is an interesting question. In the opinion of
this critic the adolescent Romeo and Juliet experienced
much more of the reality of love than the mature Antony
and Cleopatra could ever hope to know. The youthful
Jesus hardly appears to have a mature mind when he is
placed alongside an Aristotle. I do not mean, however, to
belittle either Aristotle or the mind. But while we always
allow for human finitude and frailty, the important thing

in a person is the order and direction of his loves, how wholeheartedly he gives himself to them, how responsibly he serves them with a disciplined craftsmanship, and how well such devotion may be blended with humility for himself and with charity towards others.

9

The Limits and the Powers of Love

The limit of love is sin. That is its principal negative limit. It has others. Love may conflict with duty; it may be lacking in wisdom; it may fall short of justice; it may bring more slavery than liberty; it may prove careless of inequalities because it leaps past them; it may show itself in impotence, and yet turn out to be the greatest power there is.

While this is not a treatise in aesthetics, we may pause to ask the relationship between love and beauty. There is the agonized cry of Troilus, as he watches from a corner of the stage the unfolding on center stage of the unfaithfulness of his beloved Cressida, "If beauty have a soul, this is not she." The question is not raised in *Romeo and Juliet;* beauty has a soul. The question is not raised in *Antony and Cleopatra;* beauty has not a soul. Just what, indeed, for our humanity, are the relationships of love and truth and beauty? It seems they do not always come together.

For all these relationships it can be said that they are dialectical, or that they are diversely functional. Love may undergird duty or justice; love may contradict them; love may surpass them. The tension between love and these

other values may be destructive, and again it may be creative.

All of this is to emphasize what Pelagians in ethics forget too easily: that we are man, not God. No human love
is perfect. None of us can expect to achieve an absolute
purity of heart. Indeed, there is no more terrible delusion
than that of the lover, or parent, or ruler, or reformer, who
thinks that he is motivated by a perfect love and therefore what he does is perfectly right.

Consequently for man's love, not for God's, we have this
paradox: It is love alone that justifies, but it is also love
that needs to be justified.

Sin

In the *Taming of the Shrew*, Kate complains that her
husband inflicts on her all manner of torments "i' th'
name of perfect love." This play, of course, is a comedy.
Yet Shakespeare gets some of his profoundest truths into
his comedies. If we are to go on an exegetical tear with
this particular text, we might get at least two meanings
out of it. One is that love is always accompanied by suffering. But what is being said here is probably just that the
human lover, with the best intentions, will inflict pain
upon the object of his love. No doubt Petruchio's purposes
are both satirical and disciplinary. But when he and Kate
have settled down to the routine of matrimony, will they
no longer impose torments on one another "i' th' name of
perfect love"?

In Eugene O'Neill's *Long Day's Journey Into Night*
there is a dramatically powerful portrayal of the reality
of human love and of its limitation by sin. The older
brother loves his younger brother Jamie, and wants to

help bring him up right; but he also has an unconscious drive to make his younger brother identify with him by succumbing to booze and to sex as he has. The husband loves his wife, adores her, and would do almost anything to make her happy. But because of the poverty and hardship of his early days, he is still tight with his money. So he gets her a cheap doctor when she is ill, and the doctor feeds her opiates instead of providing therapy, and she becomes a hopeless dope addict. As a mother, she loves her son Jamie, but is so obsessed with her own neurosis that she won't bother to get a report on his "consumption" and won't hear of it when he tries to tell her. As the long day of these troubled lives moves toward its foredoomed conclusion into the night, the mother's mind meanders into reminiscences of her childhood and of her happy, carefree days in the convent school. In the last line of the play she tells us what was the beginning of all her troubles. It was the day she met the man who was to become her husband, the day she fell in love.

The first time I saw this play I could scarcely resist an impulse to rise from my seat and to flee the theater, in order to escape the intolerable fatality of an ending that was doomed in advance. The next time I saw the play I experienced two revelations. The first was that this was a profound tale of our troubled human loves, as we practice them for better or for worse. The second was that, in spite of the inescapably tragic outcome, it was still love that gave a redeeming quality to all the story. And this presence of love is what distinguishes this play from so much else that we have today in the theater. So it is on a nobler dimension in *King Lear*, where we have the most terrible suffering, but where the love that was sought at the beginning is found at the end.

Because of sin, human love always needs to be justified
by a forgiving grace and power not its own. But it is love
alone that redeems.

DUTY

There is an ancient teaching that love and duty are in
opposition to one another. Love springs from the goodness of the heart. Duty is imposed upon us because of our
sinful condition. There is something of this in the Calvinists, the Puritans, the Pietists, and Immanuel Kant. In one
satire of Kant it was suggested that there is the more
merit in doing your duty the more you hate to do it. However, the conflict between love and duty is one of the basic
themes in the classical tragedies of Corneille and Racine.
This could be rephrased as a problem in the ordering of
our loves, the problem of acknowledging which love has
priority over another love. In part this may just be an
expression of the fact of man's lack of omnicompetence.
In any case it is clear that we do not always want to do
what we ought to do.

Now the Biblical teaching, as we have discovered in
recent years, does make a duty of love. This appears outrageous to Schopenhauer and to all the romantics. Nevertheless, the commandment to love is both a divine and a
categorical imperative. It is a command to the will, not
primarily to the affections. We are commanded to act in
a loving manner toward God and our neighbor. Inclination, impulse, desire, and feeling may drag their feet and
be slow in coming along. We are not supposed to wait for
them, but rather to hope that, by the grace of God, they
may in time catch up to where they ought to be. Nietzsche
called this sort of imperative, as he found it in Kant, a
"Moloch of abstraction." Unfortunately, while Kant was

eloquent on duty, he never got around to discussing the duty to love.

The relationship of love in marriage illustrates the matter. Against the sentimentalists, Emil Brunner says that the important thing is loyalty, not love. Another realist, John Dewey, would stress the value of habit, while reminding us that the habits of marriage may be as controlled yet as free and as flexible as the habits that go into playing a violin. Certainly married love derives from obedience to a duty which embraces the disciplines of loyalty and of habit. Furthermore, to reject these routine disciplines, with the pains that they may impose upon us, is to fail to discover the full dimension of the meanings of married love.

Yet again one thinks that love should surpass duty. It is our duty to go the first mile; love tells us to go another. It is the duty of the rich young ruler, as it is the duty of all of us, to obey the ten commandments. But love calls for a sacrifice beyond that. The good Samaritan, as Martin Luther King points out, does more than his duty. He has an altruism that is universal, dangerous, and excessive. The mind that can see God and the heart that is aflame with his presence will always carry us into ways of behaving that are "beyond the call of duty."

Wisdom

Jesus died for love; Socrates died for truth. Jesus died in agony; Socrates died serene. It was a young man who died for love; it was a mature older man who died for truth. Yet both died in faith—a confidence that the values they cherished were part of an immortal meaning. And Socrates confessed that what kept him faithful to the truth was his love for it; while Jesus, who spoke chiefly of love, declared that he came also to bring to men a liberating truth.

The truth of the one was a proposition. The truth of the other was a person. The idea in the proposition was reached through a process of pure reason. The idea in the person was known through an incarnation. Disciples of the one might declare, "Blessed are they that have the cosmological, ontological, and teleological arguments, for they shall know the proofs for the existence of God." Disciples of the other could affirm, "Blessed are the pure in heart, for they shall see God." Is there any connection at all between this Socrates and this Jesus, between the Hellenic and the Hebraic?

Wisdom and love are not the same affair, but they always have need of one another. Wisdom needs love as a motive and for a sense of direction. For instance, there is much of the Neoplatonist mystic in a Copernicus, and you cannot understand Darwin's attitude toward nature if you do not understand Saint Francis. In *Love's Labour's Lost*, Shakespeare shows how those who have ruled out love in order to follow learning succeed only in making fools of themselves. For if our wisdom is not guided by worthy loves, then our wisdom will be a cheap worldly wisdom, and our truths will be trivial.

On the other hand, love certainly has need of wisdom. It needs wisdom to criticize its own pretensions, to understand the object of its devotion, and to consider the means by which it is to fulfill its calling. An unwise love is too easily content with costless well-wishing and with casual commiserations. It may corrupt and enervate with compassion when what is needed is the sharp thrust of truth, or the more difficult communication of faith and hope and joy. So we are to be gentle as the dove but wise as the serpent. Or as Martin Luther King tells us, we must combine the tender heart with the tough mind.

Yet there is a sense in which love goes beyond wisdom. *Le coeur a ses raisons que la raison ne connaît pas.* At this point love makes the leap of faith; and reason, always a laggard, comes following after. There is a wisdom of books, a wisdom of science, and a wisdom of this world. Yet all this wisdom of man is an inferior wisdom compared to the foolishness of God; for the foolishness of God is the foolishness of love.

JUSTICE

One of the classical antinomies is between love and justice. In part this separates the historic emphasis of the Jew from that of the Christian. It also distinguishes, in a peculiar manner, the Lutheran tradition from the Calvinist. Martin Luther had a marvelous feeling for the reality of the God made known in Christ. Because of the love that filled him he could interpret the Bible, sing hymns, preach sermons, and make prayers in ways that still move us. But on political and institutional matters he was worse than naïve. John Calvin, on the other hand, had a wonderful appreciation of legal and institutional structures; but he had not the same intimate feeling of love for Christ and for his fellowmen. Protestants have not always managed to get Luther and Calvin together. For this reason and for others the present writing is in no sense an adequate treatise on Christian social ethics.

Certainly love is the primary imperative. Yet love all by itself may fail in justice. How often can the loving parent be unjust to the child, and how often can the loving

spouse be unjust to the life-partner! In the larger social
scene one may sincerely love the Negro, the poor, the
outcast, and demonstrate that love in personal ways, and
yet not only fail to provide justice but even obstruct the
establishment of justice. It may not be said, therefore, that
justice is love distributed. Alas! too many tender hearts
go about distributing love and wreaking injustice.

On the other hand, justice needs love to make it perfect.
There are two radical differences between the justice that
we get from the Sinico-Hindu-Hellenic tradition and the
justice we get from the Hebraic tradition. The first tradition is static and caste-ridden. The second is dynamic,
and always inclines to the underprivileged. Only when
justice is motivated by love and perfected by mercy does
it fully respect the rights of persons.

The antinomy between love and justice is stark in the
tactics we may choose for social reform or revolution. A
Marxian ardor for justice, untouched by any love of persons or of liberty, may arouse passions of hatred or re-
venge that will overthrow an established order, only to
put a new and efficient dictatorship in place of an old and
corrupt tyranny. In the company of a Gandhi or of a
Martin Luther King, however, it may be possible to liberate either a country or a people, and yet keep alive in
society a spirit of love without which any justice that may
be established is only a well-ordered system of quiet
terror.

LIBERTY

There is, indeed, a relationship between love and liberty. But there is no simple and automatic transition from
love to the very specific civil liberties that men have won
for themselves through the ages.

There are rudimentary personal liberties—freedom of choice in residence, in occupation, in travel, in recreation —that we take for granted today, but which have been denied in kinships of love. Love does not at once lead to political liberty—the right to be free from foreign domination, with the more difficult achievement of representative government in a democracy. The special civil liberties do not obviously flow from love—freedom of conscience, freedom of expression, freedom of assembly. All these specific liberties call for the exercise of intellect, the working out of laws, and the establishment of institutions.

Certainly love must cherish the moral freedom of persons. This is one of its first manifestations. So it is that God's love for man is a love which insists that man be able to exercise a freedom of responsible choice and decision. This same link between love and moral freedom informs the spirit of a democracy. With due regard for the rights of others we seek a social order in which men and women will be free from artificial restraints as they choose among possible alternatives of policy or of personnel.

Love also lies at the root of our spiritual freedom. This is that freedom sought by the sages and seers of all nations at all times. It is freedom from the bondage of circumstance, sin, and death, and freedom for the life of love, joy, and peace. Without this spiritual freedom, all other freedoms are a mockery. How may we come at it?

In *The Tempest* Shakespeare exhibits three kinds of liberty. There is the utter liberty desired by Ariel, but this is for spirits, not for men. There is the carnal liberty sought by a Caliban, which frees him from one master only to put him into servitude to a worse. Then there is the liberty discovered by Ferdinand and Miranda, which is liberty in the bondage of love. For it is only love that liberates.

Yet it must be love of a worthy object, not of an unworthy. If it is love of the highest object, which is God, then we can understand what Saint Paul means when he tells us that we are slaves to Christ and at the same time made free in Christ. We are made free by Christ's love freely given to us, and made free by the bondage of our love to him.

EQUALITY

Love and equality, like love and liberty, have a curiously dialectical relationship. On the one hand love may contemn equality because it has a fellowship in spite of inequalities. On the other hand love may be the spring for the establishment of equalities.

The equalities that we cherish in a free society are plural and specific. There is no such thing as equality in general, any more than there is liberty in general. But there is equality before the law, as ancient as Deuteronomy. There is political equality, in the right to vote and to hold office. There is equality of educational opportunity, equality of economic opportunity, equality of vocational opportunity. There is also equality of races and equality of sexes, so far as differences of race or of sex should not bar persons from the previously listed equalities. It is characteristic of these assorted equalities, like our assorted civil liberties, that they can be legislated. Indeed, they must be enacted into law.

On the other hand love cannot be legislated. Or let us say, there is only one Supreme Legislator who can command that we should love one another. The relationship between love and equality has been put in an aphorism by Reinhold Niebuhr: "Equality is love in terms of logic; it is not love in the ecstatic dimension." Certainly it is a great convenience that particular rights of man can be made effective by the laws. But let us not delude ourselves here. There can be a perfectly egalitarian society in which the only things missing are fraternity, brotherhood, community, and love.

In part, love may be the dynamic that makes for the breaking down of barriers. So of a Saint Francis in his love for the poor, of a John Woolman in his love for the black man. It is this dynamic which is the subversive force in the way the love of Jesus cuts through barriers of sex, race, nation, hygiene, religion, and social status, although his love does not ostensibly mean to destroy those barriers.

In part we have love in order to cope with ineluctable inequalities that are always with us because of inevitable differences in function in society. So when the apostle tells us, "Wives, be subject to your husbands . . . Husbands, love your wives . . . Children, obey your parents . . . Fathers, do not exasperate your children . . . Slaves, give entire obedience to your earthly masters . . . Masters, be just and fair to your slaves,"[1] he is not trying to put a sanction on specific inequalities. He is simply trying to instruct us how love must leap over these barriers and establish a Christian fellowship both in spite of them and because of them.

POWER

Love is power, but love is not all-powerful. Here is a brother, trying to help a sister, and reaching out to her in love, with the help of every insight and discipline that his Christian faith can give him, and yet at the end he con-

fesses in defeat, "I can't reach her." It was the same with
the love of Jesus. He offered that love to all men and all
women. There were those who received that love and
rejoiced in it. There were others who perceived its meanings, and hated it. So the greatest symbol of love in history was crucified on a high hill between two thieves.

Nevertheless, love can be a great power in the life of
a person. For love lies at the root of all courage. Aristotle
writes much about courage; warns us against cowardice
as against foolhardiness; says that courage is only for
fighting men, and not for women, children, sick folk. If
Jesus does not speak directly about courage, it is because
he sees courage in a wider and deeper context. Actually
we are brave only so far as we love; for we are sustained
in courage only insofar as we love truth, or justice, or our
home, or our country, or our God.

Love is also a power in history. If it is not all-powerful,
it may yet be the greatest power. When Bertrand Russell,
an agnostic, wrote his book on power, he asked himself
who were the most powerful men in the record. In his
answer he named three men: Jesus, Gotama, Galileo. The
last named was simply chosen as a symbol for the power
of science in history. The other two were religious leaders,
apostles of love and of compassion. They are called powerful for the quite objective reason that no other persons
have influenced so many people over so great an extent
of territory for so great an extent of time. So it is that the
power of love may be crucified, yet death has no domin-
ion over it.

Indeed, it is only love that is lord over death. In Christian symbolism God gave his only-begotten Son to death
that through that Son he might triumph over death for
man. As for us, when we confront death, either we are

dreadfully alone with the loneliness of those who have never loved, or else we are sustained by the loves that have enriched our lives—a love of family, a love of country, a love of all excellence, a love of him who is our Creator, Sovereign, and Redeemer. Then shall we say in confidence, "Yea, though I walk through the valley of the shadow of death, I will fear no evil: for thou art with me; thy rod and thy staff they comfort me."[2]

10

The Allies of Love

Those who think of love in absolute terms might prefer a simpler organization of the data considered in the previous chapter and about to be considered in this one. They might claim that liberty, equality, justice, power, are to be seen as the fruits of love, and that humility, patience, purity, and joy are merely aspects of love. Part of the reply to such a claim is that values such as justice, wisdom, duty, power, can in fact be present where love is not, and that love can be present when these values are absent. That is not true, however, of the values to be looked at in this chapter. Indeed, it can be said that, if these are absent, then love is absent; if love is present, then these are present.

In a way, then, we are about to examine some of the marks of love, some of the tests of its reality. In any case it is advisable, for practical reasons, to be rugged pluralists in our consideration of moral and spiritual values. For while we insist here on the primacy of love, the danger of making it an absolute is that soon we shall be thinking that, if we have love, then we need not be concerned about the rest since the rest must follow automatically. In no time, then, we shall have but an attenuated caricature of love. Because, as the apostle says, our knowledge now is partial rather than whole,[1] it is necessary to subject ourselves consciously to the discipline of checking whatever love we claim to possess against the claims of wisdom, justice, and power, and of gratitude, contrition, humility, patience, purity of heart, and joy.

GRATITUDE AND CONTRITION

Reinhold Niebuhr has said that the two basic religious emotions are gratitude and contrition. They are the conditions that liberate love within us. When we "get religion" we begin, not with a reason, but with an attitude.

Gratitude springs easily from the uncorrupted heart. Little children have it by nature, but an adult may need divine grace to recover what was once natural to him. The religious man is grateful because this is his Father's world. He loves God because God first loved us, and made his covenant with us. Every day such a man can be grateful for the good things in nature—for field and stream, for the splendor of the sea, the majesty of the mountain, the spacious glory of the heavens—and for all life that swims, or walks, or flies therein. He can be grateful for what he finds in human nature—for tokens of love and joy and faithfulness, for the courage that rises to heroic endeavor and for simple loyalty to the daily task. He can be grateful also for every excellence he finds in labor, in marriage and the family, in government, in learning, the arts, and the sciences, so far as these express the creative spirit of God as it works in man.

Gratitude is in inverse ratio to affluence. The more we have, the more we complain that this is really not so good as we deserve. When we have only a little and come by it

with difficulty, then we can be grateful for small favors
and humble satisfactions. It is not Puritan austerity but
hedonistic abundance that has driven gratitude from our
hearts. Gratitude is also in inverse ratio to pride. It is more
pleasant to think of what others owe us than to acknowledge our indebtedness to them.

All this may mean that we need to learn better one of
the lessons that suffering can teach us. As for myself, much
to my astonishment, it was not until I was serving as a
chaplain on an attack transport in World War II, on the
eve, as I thought, of a dangerous landing operation, that
I first appreciated the simple temper of praise and of
gratitude in the Psalms. As for our Lord, if it is true that
"love is gladdened by goodness,"[2] he could be gladdened
by it, even as he hung on the cross, in the repentance of
the second thief.

Contrition as a primary emotion is opposite to our
whole modern tendency to find a scapegoat everywhere
but in ourselves for what goes wrong with this world. So
we are disposed to blame it on our parents, or our siblings,
or the system, or the establishment, or the capitalists, or
the communists, but never on the things we have done
that we ought not to have done nor on the things we have
left undone that we ought to have done. Contrition
springs in part from an awareness of how little we deserve
the many good things that have been heaped upon us. It
comes more deeply from a realization of how readily we
explode into self-righteous ranting and rioting with energies that ought to be disciplined to the specific tasks of
personal reform and of social reconstruction.

Contrition has nothing to do with the luxurious cultiva-
tion of guilt feelings. Of course there are countless persons who need to discover a sense of guilt. But so long as

we are obsessed with our own guiltiness, we are thinking first of ourselves, not of the other person; we shall probably fall into extreme behavior by way of overcompensation; and we are more concerned to purge our own breast than to give help to another. This wallowing in guilt feelings is the act of the spiritual voluptuary.

A Christian knows for sure that he is a sinner. He is also thankful that his sins are forgiven. Having this gratitude and this contrition, he then steps forward to an act of faithful commitment in the service of a task that requires to be done. This calling he accepts in the spirit of love to God and to his neighbor.

HUMILITY

Humility and true love walk hand in hand. When Romeo thinks himself in love with Rosaline, his attitude is predatory and exploitative. When he falls utterly in love with Juliet, suddenly he finds a new mood of humility and even of awe.

Let it be confessed, however, that a false humility can be put to base uses. So Brutus, thinking of Julius Caesar, says that "lowliness is young ambition's ladder," but that, once the top rung has been reached, the ladder is cast away. Friedrich Nietzsche, with a more diabolical insight, saw humility as the small man's device for getting even with the big man. Here it is the instrument of the egalitarian who likes to speak in self-deprecation of "poor little me," and who is resolved to drag others down to his own level so that they, too, may become as much of nothing as he is himself.

The principal attack on humility comes from two directions. There is the proletarian, or Marxian, attack, which says that humility is recommended to the lower classes in order to keep them docile before the exploitations of the ruling class. There is the aristocratic attack, which puts an emphasis on the importance of self-respect. This can be found as early as Aristotle's portrait of the High-minded Man who is worthy of all good things and who knows his own worth. Spinoza is speaking in this same aristocratic, rationalistic tradition when he says that "humility is pain which arises from the fact that man regards his own want of power."

The critical question, from a practical point of view, is, Before what are we to be humble? If we are just humble before ourselves, as "poor little me" so obviously is, then humility is a mask for its opposite, which is pride. On the other hand a cringing obsequiousness before wealth, power, success, material splendor, has nothing to do with it. The humility of a religious person is rooted first of all in his gratitude and contrition before God. More than that, such a person may be humble in the presence of a great soul, or of a noble cause, or of a superior skill, or, if he has the mind to see it, before the child of God that is yet present in any fellowman regardless of how much it may be hidden by the fact of sin. So, paradoxically, the power of self-respect in a humble man derives not directly from a regard for himself but from the strength of his devotion to the excellence before which he is humble.

Who has this humility? The great man has it; the one who is merely a "big shot" has it not. The scholar is humble in his love of the truth; and, if he is a teacher, he may even be humble in his love of his students. The great men I have known in my own professions—John Dewey, Bertrand Russell, Reinhold Niebuhr, Paul Tillich—all had this humility as a personal quality; for "love makes no parade, gives itself no airs."[3] It is the part of a lesser man to put on arrogance and a snobbish show of self-impor-tance. The best beloved leader of our American democ-racy, Abraham Lincoln, had this humility to an extraor-dinary degree. Such persons may not have the High Mind intended by Aristotle; but they do have the Great Heart.

There is, finally, a curious link between humility and a sense of humor. Heathen humor is the "sudden glory" of the ego described by Thomas Hobbes, wherein I laugh at the discomfiture of another. Christian humor is shown in the ability to laugh at oneself. In this manner humor may be a discipline against pride and a school for an exercise in humbleness.

PATIENCE

"Love is very patient."[4] So wrote Saint Paul.

But who wants patience? Not the very young, and not a young country. There is a cardinal difference here be-tween America and England. Americans are proud of their impatience; they believe in getting things done. Eng-lishmen are proud of their patience; they know it takes time to get things done. American impatience easily esca-lates into hysteria; English patience too readily degener-ates into inertia.

Max Lerner has a name and a description for the American ailment. He says we are becoming a people with "no yesterday . . no tomorrow . . . With past-unus-able and future-disposable, Americans are trying to get along only with a present . . a now generation . . a today Ethos, unlimited in space, but one-dimensional in time . . . One term to apply to it would be INSTANTISM . . . The millions of people who turn to the stock-market quotations, all they want is an instant treasure-trove . . .

Others want instant victory over the enemy, instant justice, instant vindication of ancient wrongs, instant power."
And, one may add, instant sex.

James Reston shares in the same judgment, and cites
Eric Hoffer to show that this malaise is widespread in
our time: "The adolescent cannot see why he should
wait to become a man before he has a say in the ordering of domestic and foreign affairs. The backward nations,
also, panting to catch up tomorrow with all our yesterdays, want to act as pathfinders in the van of mankind
. . . There is no time to grow . . . These countries find
it easier to induce a readiness to fight and die than a
readiness to work, easier to attempt the impossible than
the possible, easier to build dams and steel mills than
raise wheat, easier to start at the end and work backward
than begin at the beginning."

To the truth that patience is one of the most difficult
disciplines for human nature we have the testimony of
great works of literature. The original folktale about Job
presented him simply as a patient man who waited it out
until he was vindicated in the end. When a great poet
took hold of that tale, he transformed Job into an impatient man who had painstakingly to discover the value of
patience. The original folktale of a King Leir also presented him as a very patient man whose virtue had its reward in due time. When a great poet took hold of that
tale, and transformed Leir into a passionately impatient
and tempestuous King Lear, he created another great
work of literature. Yet the new Lear, like the new Job,
had also to learn through suffering his lesson in patience.

A society that is unwilling to learn this lesson is largely
given over to the hotheads and the cynics. The hothead
is an apostle of instantism and also of perfectionism. He

demands that the absolute ideal come into existence at once. He does not expect to work for that ideal, but rather to achieve it by means of the grand tantrum put on with a ferocious display of self-righteousness. What the hot-head really accomplishes is to terminate whatever progress is being made, and then to feed reaction. The hothead soon converts to the cynic, who is simply a deflated hothead. Because the cynic finds that the world does not yield promptly to his urgencies, his final re-course is to turn and set about savagely smashing every-thing.

Love takes time. So far as love is in harmony with growth and lies at the heart of every creative impulse, it knows that patience is one of the supreme virtues. Pa-tience is for saints, of course; but everyone who has worn a uniform in wartime knows that patience is also for soldiers. Indeed, more than valor, it is the abiding and enduring virtue of the fighting man. Patience is also for mothers who are with child; it is for parents who bring up their children in a godly nurture. It is for all artists and creators at every level of life. Above all it is the discipline in the patience of due process that finally dis-tinguishes a democracy from a dictatorship. Patience is not mere passivity. Patience is power. Patience is the power of those who, having given all that they can of their own toward the furthering of the good, have con-fidence that providence in its own time will bring things to fulfillment.

PURITY OF HEART

The person who is pure in heart has a spontaneous and uncoerced love of the good. Mencius describes such a one: "The great man does not think beforehand of his words, that they may be sincere; nor of his actions, that they may be resolute: he simply speaks and does what is right."

The achievement of this purity of heart is not a simple thing. Emil Brunner knows this when he insists that in the sinful human condition we can never attain perfectly to such purity of intention. Aristotle has no teaching on human depravity, but perhaps he is recognizing the same problem when he makes a distinction between temperance and continence. Temperance is his name for this innate disposition to do what is exactly right. Most of us, however, manage to achieve little more than a measure of continence. Our hearts are not pure, and all sorts of evil impulses spring up from them; but we have enough of a prudent self-control to be able to smother those desires that are not in accord with the standards of morality. In other words, we contain ourselves. If we are willing to learn either from Aristotle or from Brunner, we shall realize that when anyone lays claim to a perfect purity of heart he labors under the most dangerous delusions.

Let it be added that purity of heart is much more than mere sincerity or integrity. These are qualities of wholeheartedness, let us say. And it is true that the Scriptures advise us to cut off the right hand or to pluck out the right eye if they should be an offense against the rest of the body.[5] But evil may have this integrity or sincerity of disposition. Adolf Hitler had it. And for Milton's Satan there is a stark integrity of character. Yet a brazen impurity of heart is not sanctified by its shamelessness. It is not enough just to act natural, or to be yourself. There is a difference between being honest to God and honest to the devil.

Our integrity, then, must be located in the right place. It must be an integrity of good, not of evil. And it must be an integrity in the basic values of life, not in trifles. We may not boast that we pay tithe of the mint, anise, and cummin of virtue, if we neglect the weightier matters of the law, which are justice, mercy, and faithfulness. We are not entitled to parade our taboos in eating and in drinking if we forget love, joy, and peace. The pure heart is the heart which is forever turned toward loving God with all its mind and strength, and its neighbor as itself.[6]

While the great world religions and systems of ethics differ in the detail of their definition of this virtue, they are unanimous that this purity is the source of power in living. Taoism puts it in a hyperbolical metaphor: "If a man have virtue, he is safe: reptiles do not sting him; nor do fierce beasts seize or harm him; and, if he come among soldiers, he will not fear their weapons." Mencius gives us the negative admonition: "A man must flout himself before others flout him, a house must break itself before others break it, a land must smite itself before others smite it." The last proposition of Spinoza's *Ethics* proclaims: "Blessedness is not the reward of virtue, but is virtue itself; nor do we delight in blessedness because we restrain our lusts; but, on the contrary, because we delight in it, therefore we are able to restrain them."

The Sermon on the Mount assures us that the pure in heart are blessed, for they shall see God.[7] No doubt there is a kind of circularity here. For we must love God in order to become pure in heart. Then it is that purity which enables us to apprehend the reality of his presence.

JOY

Love and joy go hand in hand. Joy finds expression not so much in speech as in song. Joy is one of the graces of love more than one of its virtues. But because joy has a radiating quality which can reach into the lives of others, it is also a virtue. This joy is both more primitive and more transcendent than gaiety. Joy springs from deep within the heart, while gaiety responds to occasions. Joy continues in being with a gentle sublimity in the midst of trials and tribulations when gaiety must fail.

There are two sorts of joy for the Christian. The first is the joy of Christmas which is a rejoicing in things natural. Here gratitude and joy are a part of one another. So a Saint Francis takes delight in created things: "Praised be thou my Lord, with all thy creatures"—with brother Sun, with sister Moon, with brother Wind, with sister Water, with mother Earth. A Charles Darwin knows this same joy, as his son Francis reports it of his father: "I used to like to hear him admire the beauty of a flower; it was a kind of gratitude to the flower itself, and a personal love for its delicate form and color." So also Julie Andrews has taught us to celebrate

> Raindrops on roses, and whiskers on kittens,
> Bright copper kettles, and warm woolen mittens . . .
> Wild geese that fly with the moon on their wings . . .
> Silver white winters that melt into springs . . .

and to see how these must be some of our favorite things. At Christmas, indeed, we rejoice in the sublime meanings that are in simple affairs, in a journey that has been finished, in food and rest that are found at the end of the day, in the faithfulness of the members of a family to one another, in the miracle and the promise of the birth of a child.

There is also the joy of Easter, which is a sort of supernatural joy. Because this is a joy which is purified and triumphant through suffering and death, we celebrate it with high hallelujahs. It is a joy which triumphs over circumstance, so that the apostle Paul, who takes part in it, can declare that he knows how to abound and how to be abased, how to be full and how to be hungry, for he can do all things through Christ, who gives him strength.[8] It is a joy that has triumphed over sin. Even though the ordeal may have broken the body, yet like Gloucester in *King Lear,* who does not learn to see truly until he has lost the sight of his eyes, one could at last lay down his life in such a manner that his heart "burst smilingly." It is a joy which triumphs over death, as, with the chorus of Beethoven's Ninth Symphony, it calls upon the "Giver of immortal gladness" to drive the dark of doubt away and to fill us with the light of day.

So it is that love's crusader, in whatever land he may wander and whatever battles he may fight, makes melody on his way:

> Fair are the meadows, fairer still the woodlands,
> > Robed in the blooming garb of spring.
> > > Jesus is fairer,
> > > Jesus is purer,
> > Who makes the woeful heart to sing.

11

The Ordeal of Love

It is in *As You Like It* that Rosalind laments, "how full of briers is this working-day world." Celia remarks, "They are but burrs, cousin, thrown upon thee in holiday foolery." And Rosalind replies, "I could shake them off my coat. These burrs are in my heart." So in romantic love there must be a measure of pain and of suffering.

Saint Paul is speaking of love in a deeper dimension when he writes about his "thorn in the flesh" which he believes was sent to keep him from grandiose ideas about himself. Just what this "thorn" was we do not know. But Paul sees it as a symbol in equation with other sufferings he must undergo because of his love of his Lord. "Hence I am well content, for Christ's sake, with weakness, contempt, persecution, hardship, and frustration; for when I am weak, then I am strong."[1] Somehow or other it is suffering which ministers to his strength.

The problem of suffering on the level of ethics is not altogether identical with the problem of evil in the perspective of theology. The theological problem, as Leibniz dealt with it in his *Theodicy,* has to do with why an omnipotent and benevolent God should have to work through suffering at all, and above all why he should allow the suffering of the innocent. The ethical approach may throw some light on the theological issue, but the ethical approach, like the Biblical, is fundamentally a practical one. We are not trying to explain suffering. We are simply asking: What should be done with it?

In any case the role of suffering is basic for Christianity, as it is for Judaism and for Buddhism. Indeed, it is interesting that the Greek word for happiness, *eudaimonia*, does not occur once in the entire New Testament. The preferred word is *makaria*, or blessedness; and this is the expression that we find in the Beatitudes. This blessedness seems to have three connotations. The blessed are those who are in favor with God. The blessed are those who know the meaning of suffering. But the blessed are also those who know the meaning of joy.

When, therefore, we say that it is love alone that justifies, but that love also needs to be justified, we are insisting that love must undergo its own ordeal. Love needs to be justified, as against hatred, by observation of the rules of the game, by its exemplification of God's law and moral order, by a discriminating regard for means and for ends, by an awareness of its limits and of its powers, by the aid of its allies or the proof of its tokens, and finally by the great ordeal which is the ordeal of suffering.

A CALL TO REPENTANCE

One of the first lessons of suffering is that it is a call to repentance. This means that suffering is sent as a punishment for sin. The idea is part of the teaching of the story of the Garden of Eden. The sin of Adam and of Eve is the sin of disobedience. The penalty imposed, after the expulsion from Eden, is that Adam must henceforth earn his living by the sweat of his brow, and that Eve must suffer pangs in childbirth.

There are those who reject the call to repentance with its promise of forgiveness. If so their suffering is the suffering of the damned, instead of the suffering that brings redemption. Shakespeare's great portrait of redemptive suffering is King Lear. It is in *Macbeth* that we get his terrible portrait of the suffering of the damned. That repentance is a live option in this play is made clear by the admirable repentance of the original Thane of Cawdor as he prepares for the death penalty for a traitor, and by the sudden repentance and acceptance of personal guilt and responsibility on the part of Macduff when he learns of the slaughter of his wife and children. Since Macbeth will not even think of repentance, his suffering takes on a truly horrible character. He discovers with a shock that he is unable to pray; he suffers from sleeplessness; his self is eaten by fear and suspicion of those about him; and at last he gives way to a spiritual weariness in which life's but a "tale Told by an idiot, full of sound and fury, Signifying nothing."

The notion that we suffer because we deserve to do so is always rejected by human pride. Most of us have an overwhelming sense of our intrinsic rectitude and virtue. So we will blame everyone but ourselves for what goes wrong—blame our parents, or the system, or the state, or God. Yet what goes terribly wrong with us in the outcome may have been in its origins the mere trifling with just one appetite in excess. One can have a taste for food, or liquor, or sex, or money, or a sensitive pride, or a foolish vanity, which seems harmless enough in itself but which, when indulged too much in time or too grossly in manner, will do injury to one's own integrity. So Hamlet speaks of the "stamp of one defect" which can corrupt all the rest of our virtues however excellent and infinite they may be. This is the "dram of evil" which may destroy all the noble substance of the self.

As human pride denies guilt, so does human folly think that the day of reckoning can be put off forever. Like Augustine, we may acknowledge a sin and appreciate its penalties, but as long as we savor the fruits of that sin, we pray to God, "Not yet! not yet!" Perhaps we have not learned that the longer the penalty is deferred, the more radical it will be.

In any case there is a basic difference here between Job and the Hebrew prophets. Job, who comes out of the experience of affluence and is akin to us, will protest his innocence, and demand to know, "Why do the righteous suffer?" When the Hebrew prophets confront a similar question from God's chosen people of Israel, their answer in effect is: "The righteous are not so righteous as they think they are. The righteous suffer because of their unrighteousness."

A CALL TO CORRECT EVILS

There is another approach to suffering which is strictly utilitarian. Here we see suffering as something to be got rid of, and try to discover its causes and cures so that we can abolish it.

An old distinction in theology makes a separation of physical evil from moral evil. The first kind derives from nature, the second from human nature. Physical evils include famine, flood, earthquake, plague, pestilence, and every kind of disease. For a long time it was thought that these evils were sent upon man as a punishment for his sins. However, with the rise of medical science and of other technologies, another attitude has developed. We now consider it our moral duty to cut down as much as possible on every kind of suffering that has a purely natural cause. In this direction, doubtless, we have made extraordinary progress, but now we begin to discover that some of the worst evils in nature today are the man-made evils of smog, water pollution, air pollution, the exhaustion of natural resources, and the defacing of natural beauty.

Moral evil is more obviously our own responsibility; and, while we learn to accept the penalty for it when it exists, we can still be industrious in trying to put it out of existence. If there is slavery, or discrimination against women, or racialism, or poverty, or war, or decay in our cities, these are evils we must attack with all the power at our command. And here it is that we have to learn one very painful lesson. It is easier to correct physical evil by an improvement in technology than it is to correct moral evil by a change in the human disposition or by a change in social arrangements. Nor may we suffer from the delusion that some new device in technology will automatically bring about a reform in morals. Better means of transportation and of communication do not of themselves make people become more friendly to one another. They may just provide occasion for an intensified mutual dislike.

So it is always needful that the reformer understand his place in history and his relationship to sin and to utopia. Because we are the children of a God who is the Lord of History, we are called upon to bear a part in every responsible action for human betterment. We are not permitted to believe, however, that, when we abolish a particular evil we also abolish sin, or that any one program for human welfare will finally bring us into the ideal society. History does allow for progress; it does not permit perfection.

This utilitarian approach may seem to contradict the approach to evil which is a call to repentance. In fact, there is no reason why both approaches and those yet to be described cannot be employed together in a variety of situations.

A CHALLENGE TO CHARACTER

At one point the experience of suffering is primarily a challenge to character. The Spartan, the Stoic, the Roman, understood this use of suffering. Suffering is an occasion to strengthen character, to prove that you can "take it," to show that you can come out of it with improved moral muscle.

The author of The Epistle of James was a hardheaded realist, who may have missed some of the subtleties of the Christian faith, but who appreciated its practical aspects. So after the inscription he begins at once: "When all kinds of trials and temptations crowd into your lives, my brothers, don't resent them as intruders, but welcome them as friends! Realize that they come to test your faith and to produce in you the quality of endurance. But let the process go on until that endurance is fully developed, and you will find you have become men of mature character."[2]

According to the actress Anne Baxter, this toughening of character through the ordeal of effort and of suffering is something we are disposed to evade in a culture in which everything appears to come easy. "There seems to be a tendency to treat life as if it is a continuation of television—just sit back and let life happen to you. Look at it when you need it, and turn it off when it's time to go to bed." The trouble with such people is that "they forget about 'the thump'—that's what I call it. That's the drudgery that goes with every job, the discouragements, the frustrations."

Many of us have been taught by a one-sided psychology that success is basic to the learning process. But there is an ancient pedagogy which says our most important lessons are learned in defeat. The most insecure are those who have always been successful. Some inward voice keeps telling them that the time will arrive when they will have to face a radical frustration, and they are not sure that they can take it. Only those who have known total humiliation can know the confidence that comes with the discovery that you can still rise again and go forward with courage. Once you have known the worst, there is no worse to fear.

Suffering is not merely to toughen character. It may be the occasion in which character moves significantly in one direction or another. Some people in suffering will succumb to bitterness, cynicism, and vindictiveness against the world. Others in suffering grow in humor, humility, in a real sense of purpose, and above all in the capacity to look upon their fellowmen with charity and with compassion.

A CHALLENGE TO COMPASSION

The curious thing about compassion is that it not only brings solace to the suffering of another, but that it brings healing to the suffering of the self. Buddhism rests upon this insight. Schopenhauer appropriated it as one of the three means of salvation permitted in his pessimistic view of life. If we can pierce the veil of Maya that separates one person from another, and realize that we are all one in a common lot of suffering, then we can be rid of our selfish individuality, find healing in the knowledge that our hurt is not unique to us, and so discover the blessedness which lies in giving rather than receiving compassion.

As a wartime Navy chaplain I had once to announce to a family the death in battle of an only son. When the grandmother opened the door to me, a stranger, and spotted the gold cross on my sleeve, she guessed at once my message before I had spoken a word, and began a tragic wailing that went on through my visit. The mother and her daughter took the news with a deep and more controlled grief. The father simply sat in his chair and said nothing. A few days later the mother called me to come and give help to her husband, since he would not eat, would not go to work, would not lie down to rest. When I came back he was sitting in the same chair, as though he had not moved from it all that time. I did not know what I could do for him. But as we talked, I discovered that he was a male nurse at an institution that cared for victims of battle shock or war fatigue. I suggested that he should go back to work, and look on these other lads as his own sons to whom he should minister in place of the son he had lost. He did go back, and found healing for himself while he gave it to others.

Paul Malte reminds us, however, that this business of sharing in the suffering of others is not always easy, and often brings disillusionment to social workers, psychologists, pastors, and teachers. "Many sufferers do not like to be helped. They want to sit in private corners, nursing along their pains. They resist—for to accept help means admitting weakness, and who wants to admit that he is weak and unsuccessful? The only Person who ever loved with no strings attached was crucified for his love —his love disturbed people. And when you share suffering you often confront the same opposition head-on. To overcome that resistance and for steady motivation a resource is needed, a superhuman supply of love when you aren't loved in return."

A Challenge to Creativity

Suffering also can be what provokes us to significant creativity. One of the great prophets saw this as the calling of the people of Israel.[3] Surely the Jews have been the most long-suffering, the most continuously suffering, of any people we know in the historical record. Everyone has had a hand in defeating, exploiting, or destroying the Jews: the Egyptians, the Philistines, the Syrians, the Assyrians, the Babylonians, the Persians, the Greeks, the Romans, the Christians. Except for the very recent instance of the new Israelis, the Jews have never had a superiority over their neighbors in power that was political, or military, or economic, or technological. Yet the facts are plain that these same Jews have produced, way out of proportion to their number, persons of distinction in finance, commerce, music, literature, the arts, the physical sciences, the learned professions, law and government, and, of course, philosophy and religion. Is the Jew, then, the great failure in history, or is his the big success story?

The prophets knew that nations as well as individuals will resist the suffering which is both an occasion for creativity and an inevitable ingredient of it. Yet all of us must at some time learn this lesson. Childbirth and parenthood are experiences in creativity in which the suffering is overborne in the joy of creation. The artist who writes a poem or paints a picture, the minister who is a shepherd to his flock, the good citizen who works for the welfare of his community, the entrepreneur who brings us new goods and services, the statesman who labors for the building of a republic in which liberty and justice are for all men, all these participate in a sacrament of suffering.

Saint Paul understood this well enough that he could boast of his sufferings—his prison sentences, the number of times he was beaten or stoned, his experience of shipwreck, the many occasions he had to face death. Indeed he viewed this suffering as a constituent element in the paradox of the calling of a Christian: "Called 'impostors' we must be true, called 'nobodies' we must be in the public eye. Never far from death, yet here we are alive, always 'going through it' yet never 'going under.' We know sorrow, yet our joy is inextinguishable. We have 'nothing to bless ourselves with' yet we bless many others with true riches."[4]

Martin Luther King became acquainted early with this paradox in the calling of the cross. Some years before his martyrdom he wrote, "I have known very few quiet days in the last few years. I have been imprisoned in Alabama and Georgia jails twelve times. My home has been bombed twice. A day seldom passes that my family and I are not the recipients of threats of death." What all this taught him was "the value of unmerited suffering" as it compelled him to make the basic choice "either to react with bitterness or seek to transform the suffering into a creative force . . . If only to save myself from bitterness, I have attempted to see my personal ordeals as an opportunity to transfigure myself and heal the people involved in the tragic situation which now obtains. I have lived these last few years with the conviction that unearned suffering is redemptive."

And this give us one more answer to the question, "Why do the righteous suffer?" They suffer in order that they may be more creative servants of the Lord.

THE MEANING OF THE CROSS

There is an episode in the early career of Jesus that has overtones of a comic irony. King Herod has just heard of the new prophet from Nazareth whose doings are being noised abroad. To his guilty and suspicious mind there can be only one explanation: "It is John, whom I beheaded: he is risen from the dead." To be sure, there was no doubt that the head of John the Baptist had been chopped off. This had been performed on the order of the King, and the head had been brought before him on a platter. And yet, you can't be quite sure about these prophets of the Lord. You may think you've done for a man with a proper execution, but somehow he refuses to stay dead.[5]

The crucifixion and the resurrection of Christ have profound meanings for a high Christology, but they have two irreducible meanings for ethics that are to be grasped here.

The good is not cheaply bought.

All goods come at a price. The chief good comes at the highest price. Even though it may have come to us initially as a free gift of grace, it is not ours in permanent possession unless we are prepared to pay the price for its keeping. The cross with the body of our Lord nailed to it is the reminder of that price.

The highest price we can pay is not just a price in money. Indeed, it has been said that a cynic is someone who knows the price of everything but the value of nothing. Who, then, is it that knows the value of everything but the price of nothing? Is it not the affluent American? He cherishes the noblest values; he has simply forgotten what they cost.

I am myself a kind of Quaker at heart when it comes to the liturgies of the church. Yet there was a Communion meal at which I presided which I have never been able to forget. Our attack transport was traveling down the inland sea of the Philippine Islands on a Sunday morning, shortly after the liberation of those islands. All about us was an amplitude of peace and beauty and joy. But as we broke the bread and drank the wine, we understood better than ever how love and liberty and joy and peace come only at the cost of the body that is broken and the blood that is shed.

The good is not easily defeated.

What the Christian celebrates finally is an empty cross, an empty tomb. Herod was right in his suspicions. You may slay the lover; you cannot kill the spirit of love. Indeed, love somehow or other gathers strength from suffering, rises again in power from a crucifixion, so that the cross in history is a symbol not of defeat but of triumph. It is not the end of the story; it is the beginning.

One of the obscene moments in American history took place right after the death of Martin Luther King. How many white men as well as black men celebrated that

death by shouting, "King is dead! Love is dead! Let violence reign forever!" So also some two thousand years ago,
with the death of another king there were those who
exulted, "Jesus the King is dead! God is dead! Love is
dead! Let hatred and oppression reign forever!"

Nevertheless, just as there are those who looking back
on history can see more truly, so there are those who at
the moment can discern more faithfully. As friends
gathered around Coretta King in a room of her own home
to console her for her loss, it was Jesse Jackson who
spoke to her, "Remember, it's not the crucifixion, it's the
resurrection that counts."

12

The Self and Its Loves

The command to "Know thyself!" was one of the principal teachings of Socrates. But the question remains: Just what are you trying to know when you know yourself? What Socrates meant is obviously in contradiction to most of the emphases so popular today. It is true he believed you could find yourself by introspection. But what are you looking for when you look within?

Not a jumble of sensations and ideas, not a burst of impulse and feeling and intuition, not a collection of willings and wantings and wishings, not a congeries of synapses and of conditioned reflexes, not a pyrotechnical trip to a world of fantasy and hallucination. What Socrates sought within the recesses of recollection were certain eternal values—Truth, Beauty, Goodness. It is only when the self knows these that it knows itself. In brief, the true self is made up of universals.

In this writing we have been discussing the great universal which is love. We are now to conclude the discussion with ten propositions which define and characterize the self in terms of its loves.

1. *The Self IS its loves.*

If someone makes the simple request, "Tell me all about yourself," how do you make an honest answer? It would not be a fair reply to say, "Look me over, kid, I'm all here!" What is all here in the physical sense is not the object of the inquiry. The person who asks the original question can form his own estimate of your height and weight, can tell the color of your hair and your eyes, can assess the style of your dress and deportment. He still wants to know about you.

A truly revealing answer is an answer that tells about your loves. When you speak of the objects of your loves, then you are really talking about yourself. Of course there are various expressions that are possible here, and they are grouped into two languages. There is a secular tradition, from Aristotle to John Dewey, which talks about interests and activities. There is an ancient religious tradition which talks about loves, loyalties, commitments, and concerns. There is no good reason to promote a quarrel between the two traditions. Doubtless there are differences in degree when I say that: I am interested in tennis, I play tennis, I love tennis, I am absolutely devoted to tennis. In any case the tennis is an important part of me. The secular language may have a kind of advantage that is practical and pedagogical. Activities indicate specific patterns of behavior which are amenable to denotation and control. The religious language, however, expresses a more radical commitment. An interest may be mild, an activity may be mere habit, but a love is all-out.

Ordinarily each love and each interest will entail its own activities. We need to remember, however, that there

THE SELF AND ITS LOVES

are assorted loves to which a person can give himself.
There is a love of persons, which can be as intimate as
that of the romantic lover or as inclusive as that of the
good professional politician. There can be a love of institutions, which is very real to those who help to create
them or who faithfully serve them. There can be a love
of material things, which is real to the sculptor, or the
engineer, or the truck gardener. And there can be in some
persons a powerful love of abstractions—Truth, Beauty,
or Liberty. In any case the self is defined by its loves.

2. *The self is LOCATED where its loves are.*

Let us beware of the fallacy of simple location. If someone, pointing to a person, asks, "Is he really all there?"
then the correct answer for that person's self is, "No, of
course he is not." To be sure, the body is there, but that
is only a part of the self. It may be, if you wish, a focal
point in the self, but it is not the only focus. The self exists
in a field of interacting energies with plural foci. The
body is one focus, but the other foci are the various objects of the loves of the self.

There is no reason why we should hesitate to appropriate for psychology the sort of field theory which has
been so fruitful in physics. Just where, for instance, is the
location of the black of the blackboard? A certain kind
of realist would say that the black is in the blackboard.
A subjectivist might argue that the black is actually in
my eye. Still another party might point to the importance
of the surrounding atmospheric conditions and of the
light that travels between the eye and the blackboard.
Now in fact the color is located in the whole field of
interaction, which involves at least a subjective focus, the
eye, an objective focus, the board, and the intervening

media of light and atmosphere. For an experimental science an object is located wherever we can get at it. It is easy to prove that the color can be got at by manipulation of any of the foci or media specified. This is not to say that the color is all over the place. But neither is it simply in my eye, or on the board. It has a complex location in a field which, however, is subject to precise delimitation.

Of course the self, like the color, must include much of what we think of as empty space. Yet I am where my loves are. If a child loves its doll, and the doll is broken, then the child's self has been hurt. If a mother loves her son, and her son is slain in battle in a far-off land, then something vital has happened to the mother's self. So also if I love my country, or my god, or my girl, and if there is defeat for the first, or loss of faith in the second, or disillusionment with the third, then something radical has happened to me. I am where these things are.

3. *The self CHANGES with its loves.*

There is no desire here to put on parade the principles of theoretical physics. But if physics has already rejected a naïve materialism in its explanation of matter, surely we ought to be ready to do the same in our understanding of persons.

In the old-fashioned solar-system model of the atom, it was assumed that the atom consisted of a central nucleus around which there revolved in a series of orbits various electrons. These electrons had the capacity to leap unexpectedly from one orbit to another, and to do so presumably without ever occupying the intervening space. Incidentally the better part of the atom appeared to be made up of just that empty space. In any case the character of the atom was determined by the relationship between the nucleus and the several electrons in orbit about it.

Once again the self is just such a complex field of interacting energies. The body may be likened to the nucleus, and the objects of our interest or of our love are like the electrons in orbit. Some of these objects in orbit—like my job, or my god, or my girl—may make their first appearance only on the periphery of the self. Some of them will leap altogether out of the orbit of the self, while others will suddenly leap toward a more central orbit, or even—in the case of a radical commitment—blend into the very structure of the nucleus itself. So it is in marriage when two persons are made "one flesh."

The self then can be changed by the development of new acquaintances, or by the awakening of new interests. The self can undergo radical conversion when it expels an old love from orbit and takes a new love to enter into the very center of its being.

4. *The self always ACTS OUT OF SELF-INTEREST.*

Obviously it is tautologous to say that the self acts out of self-interest. There is no other way it could act. Its interests are what its self is.

Unfortunately the kind of discussion that develops here tends to assume that this same self-interest is either something very immoral, or else it is something quite enlightened and hardheaded compared to a policy of utter selflessness. But why is it that a person or a nation that consciously acts just for what can be got out of it usually ends up by defeating its self? And why is it that policies proclaimed to arise from an enlightened self-interest so often turn out to be stupid and shortsighted?

The important thing, as Dewey points out, is the kind of self in whose interest you are acting. What sort of self-image has the person or the nation? In a strict sense there can be neither selfishness nor selflessness. But there can be a narrow self or a generous self, a static self or a growing self. Ordinarily we shall call selfish a self that is static, that has a narrow range of interests, and that refuses to accept the full range of implications of its interests. We shall call unselfish a self that is growing, that has a wide range of interests, and that is generous in its commitment to all the implications of its vital concerns.

Here too there is a connection between the self and happiness. Quantitatively, the wider the range of our interests, the more stable is our happiness; because, if something goes wrong with one interest, there are others to fall back on. Qualitatively, the more our loves and commitments have a spiritual quality to them, the more stable is our happiness, because these are loves that cannot easily be taken away from us. By the same token a capacity for friendship enhances happiness, because in friendship our sorrows are divided while our joys are multiplied.

5. *The QUALITY of the self depends on the quality of its loves.*

When we speak of a generous or a narrow self, of a growing or a frozen self, we are already speaking of the quality of the self. It is helpful also to make use of a distinction which is as old as Plato and as new as John Stuart Mill and which, incidentally, includes the classical Epicureans. This is the distinction between higher and lower values.

There are pleasures that are related to physical objects;

there are others that involve intellectual activity; and there are others that are moral, social, or spiritual in character. There is no desire here to belittle what used to be called the carnal satisfactions. But the satisfaction of our basic needs in food, clothing, sex, and shelter on a purely elementary level is stark indeed. It is only when such needs enter into relationships that are fully moral, social, and spiritual that they can minister to growth and also enrich the self. Once again we need to consider with Aristotle whether the loves of the self, while acknowledging the vegetable and the animal in us, also do honor to what is uniquely human in our makeup.

Besides the distinction between higher and lower loves, there is also the distinction between loves that are clear or confused. So many of us have an assortment of honorable loves—of our friends, of our work, of whatever increment of truth or beauty or justice we can help bring into the world. But we also have a set of not quite acknowledged loves—of power, of prestige, of possessions—which sneak up from the subconscious to distort or to corrupt the activities by which we serve our higher loves. Here, indeed, we need to know our selves honestly in terms of our real loves, and to see that all is ordered in an appropriate hierarchy.

Incidentally it is this quality of the loves of the self which is so crucially unpredictable about any person. We can observe his height and his weight; we can measure his I.Q.; we can chart his personality; we can note his skills and make a record of their performances. But what are his loves? Does he himself really know? All the intelligence and talent and personality in the world, if prostituted in the service of ignoble loves, will yield only a bitter fruit.

6. *The self FINDS itself by LOSING itself.*

Today it is very much in fashion for a person, or even for a nation, to be undergoing an identity crisis. Actually since time immemorial this has been part of the growing pains of an individual or of a people. We manage to make it worse, however, with the grotesque teaching that you must first learn to accept and to love yourself before you can love another. So we turn into a cause and a condition what can only be an outcome. For until you have learned to love another, there will be no self of your own to accept or to love.

Man cannot serve both Freud and Frankl. It is one thing to burrow inside of yourself looking for your Me in a series of psychoanalyses that probe and explore every odd bit of dreaming or of doing in the endless and bottomless pit of your psychic past. It is quite another thing with Fichte and with Frankl and with a great Biblical tradition to ask the basic question: "What is my vocation? What task is there to which I can give myself? Where does duty call? Of what worthy loves am I capable?" The first procedure is as profitable as diagnosing a stomachache by laying out on a table before you all thirty-two feet of the intestine and inspecting carefully every inch of it. The second procedure may seem abrupt and peremptory, but it gets at once to the essential.

Recently a very talented and attractive young lady by the name of Mimi Farina exclaimed to the public, "This is a very hard world in which to take yourself seriously." The answer to that must be: "For heaven's sake, don't take your self seriously—not that narrow and constricted little self. Take it only with humor and with humility. Take seriously your God, or your job, or your neighbors, a passion for truth or for beauty, some purpose of social justice, an occasion for mirth or mischief with friends, the unspoiled sense of wonder at the world in a little child—take seriously these things, learn to fall in love with them, and your self will be added unto you."[1]

7. *The self finds SELF-CONTROL in SELF-SURRENDER.*

Most great systems of ethics, whether Epicurean or Confucian or Stoic or Aristotelian, believe in the importance of self-control. The big question is how to attain to it. The classical answer in philosophy is that reason is the instrument to control impulse, appetite, and desire. Some Protestants, feeling the inadequacy of this same reason to meet its responsibilities, have denounced self-control as an instance of "salvation by works," and have moved almost to the point of promoting a Christian libertinism.

Nevertheless, when Saint Paul gave his enumeration of the nine gifts of the Holy Spirit, while he began with "love, joy, peace," he concluded with "self-control."[2] A Christian, therefore, must certainly practice and exhibit self-control. But it does not come to him simply from his reason. This power of self-control is the consequence of an initial act of self-surrender to the God revealed in Jesus Christ. Because the Christian apprehends this God in faith, follows him in hope, serves him in love, the Christian is able to regulate all other impulses that may beset him. For it is finally not reason with its reasons but the drawing power of a great love that enables us to order and to control all lesser loves and appetites. Because we love dearly in one direction, we are not so easily tempted to another.

This, indeed, is the practical meaning of salvation by faith rather than by works. The commitment of hope and love must precede the works, or the works won't really work. Self-control that is not rooted in an initial self-surrender can only multiply a fussy officiousness before it falls into confusion.

8. *The self is RELATED TO OTHER SELVES by shared loves and activities.*

With all our contemporary obsession with communication and with involvement, one must wonder if what has happened is that we have simply lost the clue to the way in which people really communicate with one another and get involved in each other. For we do so basically by shared interests, activities, loves, loyalties, concerns, commitments.

Nor is there any magical device, by way of sensitivity-training, or tactile liturgies, or "eyeballing," or all getting together nude in a sauna bath, that can bring us close to one another in any significant sense. A shared activity in home-making, or in going to the theater, or in battling for a cause, or in worship, or providing occasions for friendly intercourse and discourse—this can do something to bring out selves, to unite them, and to distinguish them, to help them to grow, and to enable them to find meaning in life. What is scandalous in our popular therapies is the way they trivialize human relations.

When we share our loves, let it be remembered that an object of such a love can be another self. So when Saint Paul writes the very personal Epistle to Philemon, he returns a runaway slave with the observation, "I am sending a part of myself," and he enjoins the master to show generosity to the runaway because "you owe your very self to me as well."[3] The last phrase quoted indicates that Paul had brought Philemon to Christ, and that he felt that the common love of Christ shared by all three of them was what united them most intimately. This kind of relationship in a shared love does not make for the facile chumminess of children, but it cements a bond that has greater depth and strength.

9. *"A CHRISTIAN MAN lives not in himself, but in Christ and his neighbor. He lives in Christ through faith, in his neighbor through love."*

When Martin Luther wrote these words into his *Treatise on Christian Liberty,* he said the essential. On the one hand, this saying puts aside the pious caricature of the Christian as one who is always probing his own bosom and inspecting his sins. The Christian knows he is a sinner and knows he is forgiven. Now his attention is turned elsewhere toward action. This means that the Christian is an eccentric as compared to all self-conscious seekers after self-realization, self-fulfillment, self-love. He is an eccentric because the focal point of his self lies outside what others think of as the self. He is also free from what John Dewey calls the cardinal fallacy in philosophy—the conversion of an eventual function into an antecedent reality. For the Christian knows that the self with which he begins is paltry enough in itself, and that he will never find an admirable self until he fixes his affections on worthy objects of love.

The Christian man does not look within himself. He looks up, and he looks out. He looks up to Christ in faith; he looks out to his neighbor in love. The upward reach of faith, the outward reach of love—these are what give definition and power to his being.

10. *The self is made IMMORTAL by its loves.*

Or else its mortality is intensified by debased loves. It is Albert Camus in *The Fall* who asks how one could conceive an immortal soul for a lascivious monkey. Indeed, if man is no better than that, if he is merely a complex pleasure-pain mechanism, if his constituent elements are only the atoms whirling in the void imagined by Lucretius, then the only decent ending is that what came out of the inane should become a thing of naught.

The philosophic clue to another vision lies in one of the arguments advanced by Socrates in the *Phaedo*. He asserts that like is known by like, and that, since the soul is that faculty in us which knows an immortal Good, then the soul itself must be immortal. What Socrates presents in a syllogism is really the expression of one of the profoundest mystical experiences of man. For if the self is given to the love of abiding and universal values and not just to an affection for what is temporal and trivial, then the self must take on the character of that which it loves and with which it is most intimately associated.

Saint Paul came upon this truth almost against his will and with an unexpected clarity as he traveled the road to Damascus. Here suddenly he surrendered hatred for love. He put off the Old Adam of sin and put on the New Christ of salvation. Writing about this experience sometime later, he spoke with eloquence of the old self and of the new self: "It is sown in corruption, it is raised in incorruption: It is sown in dishonour, it is raised in glory: it is sown in weakness, it is raised in power."[4] So it was that Saint Paul, even as Socrates, came to know that, when he turned his love toward the immortal excellence of what is man's chief good, he was already a partaker of life everlasting.

POSTSCRIPT for
Heathen Theologians

The problem for theology, as for atheology, is what be-
liefs must be held in order to support an ethics of love
and of suffering. This problem is more than can be settled
in a few pages. But here we can open up the problem, indicate certain alternatives, and make some emphases.

From a strictly empirical point of view the atheologists
are precluded from the inquiry. Since in fact they rarely
mention love and suffering, and since they therefore
offer nothing to clarify the meanings of love and of suffering, it is hardly to be expected that they should have
much wisdom about a supporting framework of belief
for these values. And surely it would be presumptuous if,
hearing by the way some word about love, the atheologists should declare that of course they have always
been in favor of such a thing, when it is obvious that they
have scarcely ever given it a thought. Once again, it is
only the great religious traditions—Judaism, Christianity,
Buddhism—which have really been concerned with the
matter.

As for such persons as are here labeled heathen theologians, they are the ones who, still calling themselves

theologians, mean to discard the belief in God which is central to any theology, or to inflate or to diminish beyond recognition the belief in Christ which is central to Christianity, or else casually to dispose of the immortality of the soul as an unnecessary appendage to their system. Most of these alterations in doctrine are proposed with a view to meeting the secular temper of our times; but it is evident that only among professional theologians is there any excitement about such notions, while there are no secularists who will pay the least bit of attention to the dispute.

The atheological theologians have proclaimed in a dramatic manner the death of God. Here at last they dare to utter boldly what was uttered two hundred years ago by Holbach and almost one hundred years ago by Nietzsche. But if their utterance has reference primarily to a trait of our culture, then it must be said categorically that they are wrong. Today it is godlessness that is on the way out. Indeed, we live at the time when atheism is at the end of its tether. Now at last atheism has been allowed a sufficient length of rope with which to hang itself. For a Sartre, life is The Absurdity; for a Beckett, life is The Mess. But an Absurdity or a Mess can yield no kind of coherent ethics. Certainly this sort of rationalism can no longer support the classical ethics of wisdom or of duty. All that is left is a senile quest for pleasures that have no yesterdays and no tomorrows, or a savage lust for power that attempts to drown in an intoxication with itself the realization of its ultimate inanity.

A seemingly more respectable—though historically heretical—device for emasculating the Christian faith is to make a big to-do about the absolute and inclusive centrality of Christ in our teaching. There are two ways to do this. One is to inflate the Christ out of all proportion to the Scriptural record, until he has fairly swallowed up God the Father and God the Holy Spirit, and resides at last on such a lofty plane that one can scarcely get him down to the cross at Calvary, not to mention trying to have him talk sense for ethics in the parables and in the Sermon on the Mount. The other way is to deflate the Christ to the size of a merely human figure, who is nevertheless the sublimely human figure, and then to talk in grandiose generalities about the Christocentric situation and Christocentric decision-making and a Christocentric ethics, while scrupulously avoiding the naïve specification of rules and of principles which made vulgar the older teaching of the "Jesus-way-of-life." These zealous manipulators of the person of Christ are the more desperate in their professed loyalty to him as they are aware that they have thrown away every other prop of the faith. The end of the matter is that, having discarded all else, they must at last lose their Christ also as he is expanded or shrunk clean out of sight.

What is offered in this brief essay is by no means an adequate theology. But it is, I am confident, a minimal theology for an ethics of love and of suffering. I put it forth as the theology of a pious positivist, of a devout agnostic. For we are up against Santayana's distinction between skepticism and animal faith; against David Hume's realization that, regardless of how the intellect may elaborate its doubts, when it comes to daily conduct we are obliged to rely upon the assurances of tested custom. Indeed, agnosticism may be admirable for the mind; it is quite impossible for the will. If we are going to act

at all, we shall act on the premises of a faith which is
supported by the probabilities of an historically disciplined pragmatism.

An ethics of love and of suffering calls for a God in
whom love and suffering are a part of his reality. This
God cannot be the God of Aristotle and Spinoza, in whom
the impersonal overrules his personality. He is better
characterized as the Lord of History, the Creator of
heaven and earth, the Judge and Redeemer of mankind.
He is likewise the true God, not one of the tin gods—
which are Nature, Humanity, Society, the Self. In fact,
in the human record, there are no other gods to choose
from except these five candidates. But the true God, who
is a God of love that knows the meaning of suffering, is a
person of power. He is the God of whom Martin Luther
King, in a moment of crisis in his own life, could say
with confidence, "Our God is able."

An ethics of love and of suffering also calls for an
incarnate logos. It is required that the word should be
made flesh. Seeing is believing. As long as love is only
a word, then philosophers might talk about it, politicians
commend it, and poets write verses about it. I myself, as
I like to think, have uttered and written some very fine
things about love. But it is not enough to speak of love
with the tongues of men and of angels. It is necessary to
have love—more than that, to be love. Otherwise all our
discourse is as sounding brass and tinkling cymbals.[1] The
Christ is he who was, who is this suffering love. So he
could say, "I am the way, the truth, and the life."[2] Yet
Pilate, looking upon him, could ask, "What is truth?"[3] not
knowing that he stared it in the face.

Finally we need a belief in the immortal worth and destiny of the human individual. Here the debate between the Greek notion of the immortality of the soul and the Jewish belief in the resurrection of the body points to important issues. We must decide if at last a person belongs in two pieces or in one. As for myself, when it comes to the pinch, I give priority in the categories of religion to the Hebraic over the Hellenic. Yet this debate should not obscure for us the larger question. Certainly for ethics it makes a deal of difference whether I see a man, or a woman, as a child of God with an eternal value, or see only an organic object which is somewhat more complicated than an ape but less efficient than a computer. The record is clear, in Lucretius and in Hobbes, that the consistent atheist, who rejects both God and the soul, cares only for an ethics of pleasure and of power. An ethics of love and of suffering gives light and might to our earthly pilgrimage because it is inspired by the vision of a heavenly city.

For religious faith, while it must undergo the discipline of reason, rests initially and ultimately on an act of creative imagination. This is not an imagination which creates out of nothing. It is an imagination which enables us to embrace a perspective of reality that is larger and bolder than one that might satisfy a more prosaic temperament. The formal test of this perspective, as of any other, lies in its adequacy to all the diversity of experience, and in its fruitfulness to enlarge and to deepen that experience with richer seeings and with nobler doings. In this religious experience love and suffering are among the primary facts of life, as are also God, and the Christ, and the sacredness of persons. We do not so much demonstrate the truth of these facts by arguments about isolable propositions, as we do take account of these facts, espouse them, and follow them through to the uttermost limit of their meanings. Only then can we enter into the secret of that life which Martin Luther King himself exemplified when he wrote of the *Strength to Love*.

References to the Scriptures

The following symbols are used to indicate which translation of the Bible has been used:

KJV—King James Version
NEB—New English Bible
RSV—Revised Standard Version

The names of Moffatt and of Phillips are spelled out when either of their translations is used. No indication is given when it does not matter which translation is used.

Chapter 1 THE CHOICE TO LOVE

1. Matthew 10:37–39, and 12:46–50.
2. I John 4:20a. NEB.
3. I John 4:20b. NEB.
4. Matthew 22:37–40. KJV.
5. Romans 7:19. NEB.
6. Cf. Psalm 86:11. KJV.
7. Matthew 4:1–10. KJV.
8. Matthew 13:22. KJV.

Chapter 2 LOVE AT WORK

1. Ephesians 5:2; I John 4:19. KJV.
2. Hebrews 11:1. KJV.
3. Matthew 7:1–5, and 13:24–30, 36–43, and 24:45–51.
4. Matthew 6:14–15, and 18:21–22, 23–35; Luke, ch. 15, and 17:3–4, and 23:34. KJV.

5. Isaiah 42:1–4, and 49:1–6, and 50:4–9, and 52:13 to 53:12. KJV.
6. I Corinthians 13:7. NEB.
7. I John 3:13. NEB.
8. Luke 12:49–53. NEB.
9. John 4:34. NEB.

Chapter 3   LOVE AGAINST LUST

1. Psalm 121:1, first in KJV, then in RSV.

Chapter 4   LOVE AGAINST VIOLENCE

1. Galatians 5:15. NEB.
2. Cf. Ezekiel 24:6–14. KJV.
3. Matthew 11:12. KJV.
4. Matthew 10:16. KJV.
5. I Corinthians 1:25–31. KJV.
6. Matthew 5:43–48; Luke 6:28–31; I Peter 3:9. NEB.
7. Matthew 5:45a. KJV.

Chapter 5   LOVE AGAINST ANARCHY

1. I Corinthians 14:40. NEB.
2. I Corinthians 2:16; Philippians 2:5. KJV.
3. Matthew 19:16–22. KJV.
4. Titus 1:5–9. NEB.
5. II Timothy 2:5. NEB.

Chapter 6   —THE RULES OF THE GAME

1. Matthew 22:11–14. KJV.
2. I Corinthians 13:4–7. NEB.
3. Jeremiah 31:33–34; Hebrews 8:10–11. KJV.
4. See the Epistle to the Galatians.

Chapter 7   LOVE AS THE LAW OF LIFE

1. Psalm 119:105, 54, 97. RSV.
2. Romans 13:7–10. NEB.

3. Romans 1:28 ff. NEB.
4. Galatians 5:22–23.
5. Ephesians 4:15. KJV.
6. Psalm 37:25. KJV.
7. Deuteronomy 30:19–20. KJV.

Chapter 8   LOVE'S MEANS AND ENDS

1. Matthew 5:21–28.
2. Matthew 22:37–39.
3. Matthew 7:17–20. KJV.
4. Matthew 25:31–46.
5. Galatians 5:19–22. NEB.
6. I Corinthians 13:13. NEB.
7. I Corinthians 13:4–7.
8. Matthew 7:21, 24, 26. KJV. Italics mine.
9. Luke 10:38–42.
10. Matthew 20:22. KJV.

Chapter 9   THE LIMITS AND THE POWERS OF LOVE

1. Colossians 3:18–25, and 4:1. NEB.
2. Psalm 23:4. KJV.

Chapter 10   THE ALLIES OF LOVE

1. I Corinthians 13:12. NEB.
2. I Corinthians 13:6. Moffatt.
3. I Corinthians 13:4b. Moffatt.
4. I Corinthians 13:4a. Moffatt.
5. Matthew 5:29–30, and 18:8–9.
6. Matthew 23:23; Romans 14:13–18; Matthew 22:37. KJV.
7. Matthew 5:8.
8. Philippians 4:4–13. KJV.

Chapter 11   THE ORDEAL OF LOVE

1. II Corinthians 12:7–10. NEB.
2. James 1:2–4. Phillips.

3. Isaiah, chapter 53.
4. II Corinthians 11:23–37, and 6:8–10. Phillips.
5. Mark 6:14–29. KJV.

Chapter 12   THE SELF AND ITS LOVES

1. Matthew 6:33. KJV.
2. Galatians 5:21–22. NEB.
3. Philemon, verses 12, 19. NEB.
4. I Corinthians 15:42–43. KJV.

POSTSCRIPT FOR HEATHEN THEOLOGIANS

1. I Corinthians 13:1–3. KJV.
2. John 14:6. KJV.
3. John 18:38. KJV.